101

YOUTH BASKETBALL

DRILLS AND GAMES

Bruce Brown

COACHES
CHOICE™

ISBN: 1-58518-313-X
Library of Congress Catalog Card Number: 2001095649
Book design and diagrams: Jeanne Hamilton
Cover design: Trisha Henderson

Coaches Choice
P.O. Box 1828
Monterey, CA 93942
www.coacheschoice.com

DEDICATION

I dedicate this book to my co-coach, partner and wife, Dana, and also to all my athletes, past and present.

ACKNOWLEDGMENTS

I am grateful to all my coaching partners and coaching opponents who have helped shape me as a person and coach, as well as influenced my career. I am also thankful for having the opportunity of sharing my love of working with young people.

C = COACH

O = OFFENSIVE PLAYER

1,2,3,4,5 = OFFENSIVE PLAYERS

○ = PLAYER WITH THE BALL

X = DEFENSIVE PLAYER

X1,X2,X3,X4,X5 = DEFENSIVE PLAYERS

PASS =

CUT OR PATH OF THE PLAYER =

DRIBBLER =

SCREEN =

Example = Offensive player O4 who starts with the ball, passes it to O2 and then screens for O3 who uses his screen to cut.

CONTENTS

FOUR KEYS TO SUCCESSFUL DRILLS

Overview

Practice has by far been the most enjoyable part of my three decades of coaching basketball. The time that coach and athletes share together in a focused teaching and learning environment provides the ultimate moments in our profession. Being part of an athlete's improvement in individual and team skills is more satisfying than the outcome of any game. Skill improvement takes place when teacher and student are both equally motivated and follow a well-prepared plan.

In order to teach complex skills, each skill must be broken down into teachable parts and drilled until it becomes instinctive. Accordingly, each drill should serve a specific purpose with your offensive or defensive system.

This book is designed to cover basketball drills specific to the varied and diverse aspects of the game. Each chapter begins with drills that are simple and then progresses toward more advanced levels of instruction. This book does not attempt to provide a complete or exhaustive list of drills, but rather selected drills that have proven to be successful with players from ages 10 through 18.

An essential point to keep in mind is that proper drilling will produce desired results. Improper drilling, on the other hand, will produce improper results. *Your success or failure as a coach can be substantially influenced by your ability to select, devise, adjust and teach drills that meet the particular needs of your team and players.* In my career, I have found that successful drills adhere to the following four keys:

Key # 1: Selecting Purposeful Drills — Choosing What You Are Going to Teach

---

- Consider your players' ages and abilities when selecting drills.

- Make sure every drill has a clearly defined purpose.

- Choose drills that are applicable to your offensive or defensive system and build them to a point where they are conducted at a speed that simulates game conditions.

- Seek (on an ongoing basis) new drills and techniques for performing specific skills that can help your players improve.

- Choose drills that are simple enough that the players are capable of understanding the techniques involved in the drill, and how the drill fits into the big picture. (Athletes will learn a new skill easier if they see the material as meaningful and useful.)

- Make sure that the drills are structured such that both you and the players can clearly discern improvement. Players will be more eager to learn when they feel that they are making progress in a drill and can see results from engaging in the drill carried over into games.

Key # 2: Teaching the Drill — Using Your Knowledge to Enhance Your Players' Performance

---

- Understand that it is not only important how much you, as the coach, know; rather, it is more important how much of what you teach the players can grasp and perform.

- Fully understand your teaching environment before you begin teaching a drill for the first time. For example, how many players do you have? How much space? How many baskets? How much time? How many coaches? How can you maximize all of these variables?

- Teach a drill correctly *the first time.* This is essential in order to maximize the learning environment for a drill. Accordingly, you need to plan and prepare so that the first time a skill in introduced you use the correct technique (modeling) and the correct terms.

- Allow adequate time for making corrections when drills or techniques are improperly performed. Having to correct things that are done poorly or incorrectly requires "unteaching" and "reteaching" which takes time and confuses the athlete.

- Demonstrate (or have someone else demonstrate) the whole picture of the drill, break the drill down into teachable parts, and then build it back into the whole.

- Emphasize the parts of the drill done correctly at increasing levels of speed as the skill level of the players improves.

- Do not expect skills to be mastered at the same rate by all the players. As the coach, you need to understand how to help athletes who are struggling with the "basics", without boring those who are ready to practice more advanced skills.

- Working in small groups that are organized according to each player's level of expertise not only allows athletes to progress at their own rate, but also gives each player more repetitions.

- Emphasize to your players that performing repetitions correctly is the primary key to individual skill improvement.

- Avoid using a drill for too long at any given time once it has been taught. For example, if you need to spend 20 minutes on a specific skill, you should consider breaking it down into two 10-minute segments or even better, four 5-minute segments. It is better to practice a skill in shorter, more concentrated bursts of activity that keep the athletes' attention and focus on perfection than to do it for so long that they lose their intensity or concentration. Note: You know you have a special team, and you understand the teaching phase of the game when they can practice for the entire time and think of nothing else except what they are doing right now.

- Emphasize small doses repeated regularly at maximum effort, for optimal results.

- Concentrate on specific areas of the game when practicing a given drill and then gradually include multiple concepts.

- When you introduce a new drill during one practice, hand out any written material that athletes can study to assist them in pre-learning the drill. Then incorporate the new drill into practice the following day. This approach tends to enhance learning and performance.

- Plan your practice so that drills that are new or require more thinking occur early in practice. Drills done at the end of practice are the ones that require execution of fundamentals done correctly while players are tired.

- Vary your drill progression within a practice session. The coach should alternate drills that are physically demanding with drills that are not as physically demanding to perform.

Once the skills have been correctly modeled, the coach should begin the next phase of the learning process, **correction** and **positive motivation.**

Key # 3: Correction — Making Positive Changes in Performance

One of the most important lessons young athletes can learn is *to be able to take correction as a compliment*. If athletes are coachable and appreciative of a coach attempting to help them, they will improve. It is equally important for the coach to develop the ability to give direct, specific correction that can be understood and accepted by the player. Correction needs to be done with a spirit of caring about the individual. This approach maintains everyone's dignity and helps the true message get through to the athlete. A coach must learn to *correct the action, not the person*. The player must understand that the coach's job is to help him become a better player and athlete. Accepting correction comes with the territory if you choose to be an athlete. Giving a correction in a manner that can be accepted by the athlete is a requirement of successful coaching.

The coach needs to have a vision of what he expects a skill (drill) to look like, and then use his coaching skills to get each of his players to that level of performance. You must have the athletes' *full attention* before you can expect improvement. The coach cannot overlook slight imperfections. You can never lose your persistence to detail. Practicing a skill incorrectly is as "habit forming" as practicing that same skill correctly. Athletes need to work on accuracy of execution *before* speed of execution. Once an athlete has mastered the technique at a slower speed, the coach should require the skill to be practiced at the level of quickness needed to be successful in the game situation.

Requirements for successful skill development:

- The coach needs to understand the skill and visualize that skill being performed correctly.

- The coach must have the full attention of the players.

- The players should recognize that they are capable of improvement and then willingly accept any correction given by the coach as a compliment.

- The players need to be willing to work through the "awkward" and "mechanical" stages of performance.

- The coach must provide enough repetitions to develop "muscle memory" so that the players can perform skills instinctively.

- The players need to be able to perform the skill at "game speed" with smoothness and coordination.

Key # 4: Motivating Your Players — Balancing Fun and Discipline

The goal of every coach should be to have spirited, enthusiastic players. The primary key to having enthusiastic players is to have an enthusiastic coach. Motivation is a basic ingredient for every successful coach-player interaction. The coach should be constantly searching for new methods to encourage and motivate his players. Your own hard work, preparation and passion for the game will be your best motivational tools. Great coaches do not relax while teaching. A sense of urgency is what separates average coaches from great coaches. This does not mean that either you or your players cannot have fun. The wise coach understands the delicate balance between fun and discipline (See chapter 10).

The following keys can help keep your players motivated:

- Refer to your players by using their name or nickname.

- Name your drills (in this book, I mainly used drill names that describe the action or techniques, but you can also name drills after college or pro teams, or your own players who have performed the drill the best).

- Pick up the pace of a drill or a practice by finding a method to make it competitive, (e.g., keep score).

- Eliminate players from practice who do not listen or try – be willing to help them with their problem at another time.

- Practice drills so they are as close to game conditions as possible.

- Find ways to measure each players' performance – one of the principles of motivation is that anything that is measured, will be performed better.

- Keep your drill times short – when drills become drudgery, players will lose focus and begin forming incorrect habits.

- Be a creative coach, always looking for a better method to teach a skill.

- Conclude practice on a fun note (See chapter 9).

- Be a "positive-demanding" teacher.

- Start on time, stay on time, and end on time.

- Have a sense of humor and let it show to your players.

- Be an encourager.

- Be willing to stay after practice and assist any player who wants extra help.

CHAPTER 1

DRILLS TO USE DURING THE SQUAD SELECTION PROCESS

As you anticipate the beginning of the season, most coaches can visualize the games and practices, as well as the skills they are going to be teaching. But in most coaching situations, before you can get to the teaching/playing phase, you must go through possibly the most difficult period of the season – **squad selection**. The more carefully you and you coaching staff can prepare for this phase of the season, the better it will be.

Squad selection is never easy. The clearer you can be to your players regarding your expectations for effort, behavior, roles, and what you are looking for in the individual players, the easier it will be for everyone involved. You need to devise a fair and unbiased method to select the players for the team. After you have identified potential players and have them all on the court, it is essential that you have planned practice according to the number of players turning out, the amount of court space available, and the number of coaches and teaching stations you have available.

It is important for you to balance the desire to give each player sufficient opportunities to show his ability, and the feeling of urgency you have to get the selection process completed and move on to regular practice. Not all of the selection process can be objective; part of selecting every team will come down to the subjective judgement by you— the coach. Drills and teaching stations must reflect both objective measures and subjective judgement opportunities for the coaching staff.

Squad selection will proceed more efficiently if you:

- Alert the players ahead of time on the drills that will be used during tryout. This allows each player the same opportunity to prepare.

- Select some drills that will demonstrate the players' ability to learn quickly. Explain to them the importance of establishing who is a quick learner.

- Have each station (if practice plans include station drills) involve the same amount of time (e.g., 35-45 seconds) so that rotation from station to station is efficient.

- Give players (whenever possible) more than one attempt on tests and record either the average or the best score they achieve.

- Provide each coach or person testing with a roster and exact instructions for administering the test that they are conducting. Observe the test to ensure that the test is being conducted as you intended.

Squad Selection – Agility Evaluation Drills

Agility is the ability to change direction without losing speed or balance. Improving an athlete's agility is generally limited to teaching him how to keep his balance when turning or changing direction. For the most part, a player will either be agile or not. A substantial part of agility has to do with coordination and strength, which can change as young athletes mature into their bodies.

Drill 1 – Defensive Slides

Objective:

- To measure agility.

Description:

Tape two marks on the floor 20 feet apart and on the signal to begin, the player stays in a defensive stance and slides back and forth to each mark as many times as he can. Do not allow the player to cross his feet. When he gets to the mark, he must touch it with the hand nearest to the line. Count the number of correct touches he can make in 30 seconds, and record the number. At least one coach must be present at this station to ensure the player being tested stays in a good defensive stance and actually touches the line, and then the coach records the final score.

Drill 2 — Quick Feet Drill

Objective:

- To measure agility.

Description:

Each player stands next to a ball on the floor and on the signal to begin, the player simply sees how many times he can touch the top of the ball with each foot while alternating his feet. Have the player's partner count and call out his score when his name is called. If the player hits the ball on the side, he will not score as high because the ball will roll away.

Drill 3 — Rope Jump

Objective:

- To measure coordination and agility.

Description:

The player being tested attempts to jump the rope as many times as possible in 30 seconds. Since this is difficult to count for a skilled jumper, it is better to have them participate in groups of three for this test so that the two players not being tested can each count separately and compare their totals before recording the score.

Drill 4 — Shuttle Run

Objective:

- To measure quickness and agility.

Description:

Measure and mark two lines 30 feet apart (i.e., the width of a volleyball court). The player begins behind the starting line and on command, makes two runs between the lines. He runs to the line 30 feet away, touches it with either hand, returns to the starting line, touches it with his hand, and then continues back to the first line he touched before turning and running through the finish line. The time stops once the player's trunk crosses the finish line.

Drill 5 — Dribble Weave

Objective:

- To measure agility and speed with a basketball.

Description:

The player being tested begins with the basketball on the baseline and on command, dribbles through a series of cones or chairs placed far enough apart that the dribbler must change direction. The number of obstacles and the distance the obstacles are apart can vary, depending on the age and ability of the players as long as it is consistent for all individuals being tested. This test requires the player to dribble down and back. Each player's performance is individually timed, and the results recorded by a coach at this station.

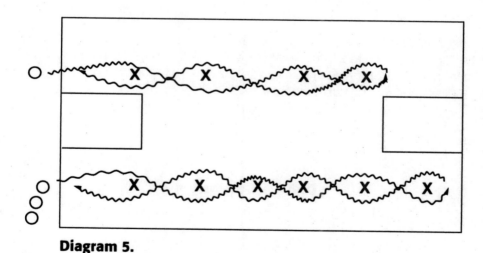

Diagram 5.

Drill 6 — Obstacle course

Objective:

- To measure speed and agility while dribbling a basketball.

Description:

With a coach at the start-finish line timing individual players, the players start at half court and follow the same path around the cones. The farther apart the cones are, the more you include speed in this test. The recorded time stops as the trunk of player's body crosses a designated finish line. If you would like to add a degree of difficulty to the drill, you can require the players to dribble with their "weak" hands or increase the number of obstacles they must circle.

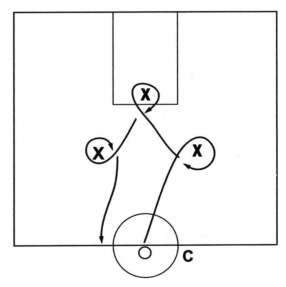

Diagram 6.

Drill 7 — Wall Pass

Objectives:

- To measure the players' wrist, hand and arm strength.

- To measure the players' ability to catch the ball.

Description:

This drill is a 30-second timed test. Depending on the age of your players, have them stand a specific distance from a flat wall and on command, see how many times they can pass the ball off the wall. The more powerfully they can pass the ball against the wall, the quicker it will get back into their hands, and the more catches they will record. The more the player has to "wind up" to make the pass or the slower the ball comes off the wall, the fewer passes they will complete. A partner or coach can count and record the total.

Drill 8 — Timed Lay-ups

Objective:

- To measure close range shooting.

Description:

This drill is a 30-second timed test. Each player is tested for his ability to make lay-ups against the clock. The player stands at a 45-degree angle underneath the basket and on the signal to start, tries to make as many lay-ups as possible. If the shot is in the air as time expires, the basket will count if it goes in.

Drill 9 — Consecutive Free Throws

Objective:

- To measure free throw shooting ability, form and consistency.

Description:

During the free throw shooting part of practice, have players divide up with an equal number at all the available baskets. Each player records the longest string of free throws he can make without a miss. Start counting on the first made shot, and rotate shooters on a miss. If a player doesn't make one of the first three attempts, then that player loses his turn. At the end of 5-to-10 minutes, record the longest string for each player. Continue to use this test each day of try-outs.

Drill 10 — Spot Shooting

Objective:

- To measure shooting ability, range, and form.

Description:

Mark some designated spots on the floor, based upon the age and ability of your players. Test them to see how many shots they can make in the circuit. Depending on how much time you have or how many baskets are available, players can attempt either one, two, or three shots from each spot before they move on to the next spot. Their score is the total number of baskets made.

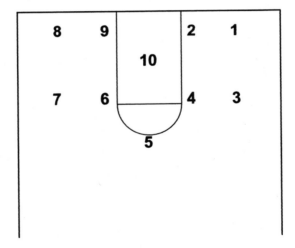

Diagram 10.

Drill 11 — Timed Shooting

Objective:

- To measure shooting ability at game speed, range, and form.

Description:

Select and mark two different shooting spots within the range of your players. Two players are responsible for rebounding the two basketballs and getting them to a passer (you could use a coach as a passer if you want, since the accuracy of the passes will effect the shooter's score). The player being tested moves from one shooting spot to the other and gets off as many shots as he can in a timed 30-second test. The coach records the total number of baskets made for each test.

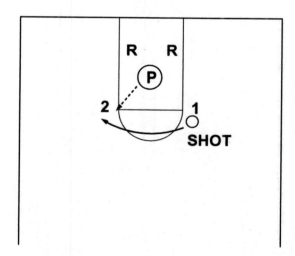

Diagram 11.

Drill 12 — Jump and Reach

Objective:

- To measure leg power.

Description:

The coach needs to place a measuring tape or similar measuring device on the wall. The player being tested stands with the side of his body against the wall, reaches his near hand as far up the wall as possible and that height is marked. The player can then take one step back from the wall and step into his jump. The player touches as high up on the wall as possible, and his score is recorded as the distance, in inches, between the two marks. Two or three jumps should be sufficient to produce a best effort.

Drill 13 — Two-Mile Run

Objective:

- To measure cardiovascular (aerobic) endurance.

Description:

This timed test can be run on a track or on a cross-country course. The purpose of the test is simple. It measures the amount of aerobic conditioning the athlete has done prior to the season. In other words it is a reflection of "how important" making the team is to the player. A coach who is going to conduct this kind of test should alert the potential team members as early as possible that it will be part of the evaluation for selecting the squad. They should also know the date the test will be given and exactly what the course will be, so that they can prepare as well as possible. In other words, preparation becomes a choice. Unless they have done the work ahead of time, they will not be able to fake it. Cross-country courses with some hills provide a better test for strength and stamina and more variety to the drill than running on a track. For players who have done the work ahead of time, the running will not be a form of punishment, but rather an opportunity to show their level of preparation and commitment.

Drill 14 — Two Ball Lay-ups

Objective:

- To measure endurance and shooting when fatigued.

Description:

This drill is a timed, one-minute test in which the coach records how many baskets the player is able to make in the allotted time period. O1 begins by picking up the ball from the floor at the left elbow of the lane and takes it strong to the basket. As quickly as he can, he goes out to the opposite elbow and picks up the second ball and takes it to the basket from the right side. He continues to alternate sides for the whole minute. A rebounder stands under the basket and passes the ball out to a player who is waiting at the opposite elbow to replace the ball just shot.

To add difficulty to this drill:

- Require that the player shoots with the correct hand on each side of the basket.

- Require that the player stay at the basket on a missed first shot until the basket is made.

- Have the athlete go until he has made 20 total shots (instead of going for a designated time period); in this instance, his score would be the time it takes to reach this goal.

- Place the balls on spots slightly further from the basket.

- Add a "net touch" or "rim touch" between each made basket.

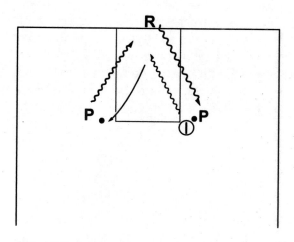

Diagram 14.

Drill 15 – 5-Man Weave Passing Drill

Objective:

- To measure learning ability.

- To practice passing and receiving.

Description:

The players get into five lines on the baseline. The first person in each line is going to work together with the first person in the other lines, going down the floor. The player in the middle line has a basketball and as all five players begin up the floor, he passes to the closest player on his right, and then circles around behind that player to the outside. The player who received the ball then passes to the closest player on his left, and goes behind to the outside of that line. Players continue to move toward the center until they have received and passed the ball, and then they move behind to the outside. If the five players are able to complete this pattern going down the floor, then challenge them to figure out how to turn around and come back. If they can successfully do that, then add shooting a lay-up at each end of the court. Next, the coach can have them complete the drill while calling out the first name of the teammate to whom they are passing.

Note: This is an example of a test that could be used to measure learning ability. One of the things that you want to test in your potential squad members is the ability to learn things quickly. While all the other tests have been posted in advance, you should save some time to teach a skill or a drill that the athletes do not know ahead of time to see who can pick things up relatively quickly and who struggles. If nothing else, it gives you some insight to the players who have different learning styles or those individuals who are going to need additional help with more complex skill learning. This learning test should be quick and easy to teach, and can be as simple as a passing drill or as complicated as an offensive pattern. As you teach it, watch to see which athletes are able comprehend and carry the instruction into action.

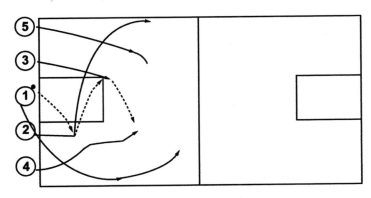

Diagram 15.

Drill 16 — Toss and Follow

Objective:

- To measure endurance, and catching and shooting skillswhen fatigued.

Description:

The player being tested starts at the foul line and tosses the ball underhanded off the backboard, follows the ball, and lays it in. Make or miss, he rebounds his own shot and hustles back to the foul line, switches sides of the basket, and repeats the action. The score that is recorded is the time it takes the player to make a total of 20 shots. This drill will test cardiovascular endurance and coordination, as the player attempts to toss the ball accurately enough to be able to follow and catch it.

Squad Selection — Subjective Evaluation

Part of selecting players for any team will come down to a subjective evaluation (i.e., comparing playing ability through activities that are not measurable). The ability to subjectively evaluate players is often what sets coaches apart. The good coach can truly see enough to justify his decision without feeling like he is guessing. The astute coach can often evaluate not only who the best players are currently, but also which players might be "sleepers". There are some players who will be able to make more improvement than others with effective coaching; some that are small now, but are going to grow later; and some that have athletic ability beyond their current basketball skills. The activity that provides the most opportunities for accurate subjective judgement in basketball is playing. As a consequence, part of every squad selection process should include the chance for each player to simply play. It is essential that each of the teams are adjusted and changed throughout to allow strong players to play together and also a time when they are required to play with less-experienced players. The best drill I have seen to evaluate playing ability is 3-on-3 half-court.

Drill 17 — 3-on-3 Half-Court

Objective:

- To subjectively evaluate half-court playing ability.

Description:

Teams compete against each other in a half-court setting. In this drill, offensive players cannot hide; they must be able to get open, operate without the ball, set and use screens, and create their own shooting opportunities. Defensively, they are never more than one pass removed from the ball. They have to be able to win their individual defensive battles and also be able to help in an open-court situation. You can choose to have the teams play at one basket, with the winning team staying and the next three coming on to challenge, or use alternate possessions or multiple baskets to win. Another method that can be used to constantly change the make-up of the teams is to have the player that is scored on leave and the next player in line replace him. That way the new player needs to be ready to come in on either team.

Drill 18 — 4-on-4 Full-Court

Objective:

- To subjectively evaluate full-court playing ability.

Description:

Having players compete full-court will allow you to see who has the open-court skills of decision making, running, catching and handling the ball on the move, and finishing, as well as defending full-court. 4-on-4 is often better than 5-on-5 in tryouts, since during tryouts, players are not usually asked to run a specific offense. It also opens up the floor, providing more chances for each player to touch the ball or guard the ball. Again, the best rotation is to constantly switch line-ups during tryouts. A way to constantly change the make-up of the teams is to have each player guard the player guarding him and rotate out if his opponent scores. The following diagram shows 4-on-4 full-court with O3 scoring. As a result, X3 leaves the court and goes to the end of the line, and the new player coming in matches up with O3.

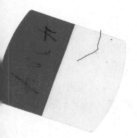

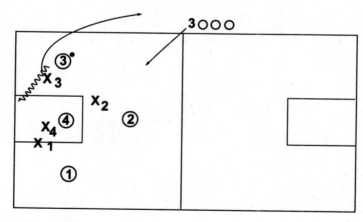

Diagram 18.

CHAPTER 2

REBOUNDING DRILLS

Drill 19 — Move Under the Ball

Objectives:

* To practice rebounding by moving to the ball.

* To practice catching the ball at its highest point.

Description:

This drill is designed to teach players to move to the basketball while it is in the air. Players get a partner with one ball for the two of them. Player O1 tosses the ball 12-to-15 feet in the air off to one side of his partner, O2. O2 begins in a defensive stance, and as the ball is tossed in the air, he moves as quickly as he can until his feet are directly under the ball before it comes down. He catches the ball directly over his head with his arms fully extended. He then tosses for his partner. This drill helps players get into the habit of moving their feet, rather than reaching to the side for the ball. Only 60 seconds (about 8 – 10 reps for each player) need to be devoted to this drill.

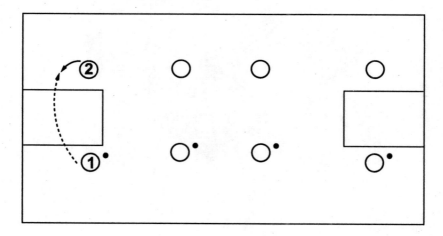

Diagram 19.

Drill 20 — Toss, Move, Jump, Chin the Ball

Objectives:

- To practice moving under the ball and catching the ball with extended arms.

- To practice protecting the ball from a defender.

Description:

As in the previous drill, players get a partner and a basketball. In this instance, the player moving to the ball quickly gets under it with his feet and jumps, attempting to catch the ball with fully extended arms at the height of his jump. After catching the ball, the player rips it to his chin level, with his elbows out and his hands pushing in from the sides of the ball. The terms used to remind players to do those two concepts are "chin it" and "leave fingerprints on the ball". As a general rule, no more than one minute is required to get enough repetitions.

Drill 21 — Get Contact, Rip, Chin and Pivot

Objectives:

- To practice making contact.
- To practice releasing to the ball.
- To practice rebounding and protecting the ball.

Description:

The two players in the previous drills now join another group of two to make four players and a ball. On the coach's whistle, O1 tosses the ball 12-to-15 feet in the air toward O3 and O4, favoring one side. If he tosses toward O3's side, O3 moves into O4 and gets contact with his shoulders, releases, and gets his feet under the ball, rips it out of the air, and chins it. After O3 has gotten possession of the ball, O4 goes after him trying to circle him and slap at the ball. O3 must pivot and protect the ball by keeping O4 behind him while strongly "chinning the ball". After a few seconds, the coach blows his whistle, and O3 tosses the ball high toward O1 and O2, who then follow the same procedure.

Key Points:

- The rebounders need to get their feet shoulder-width apart to provide a good base.
- The rebounders must maintain a lower center of gravity than their opponent, who is behind them.
- The rebounders' arms should be wide, at shoulder height, and bent at the elbows, with their hands up.
- Players should exert pressure with the balls of their feet.
- The rebounders should release from their opponent quickly, move to the ball and get their feet directly under it.
- When the players are pivoting to protect the ball from their partner, they need to keep their bodies flexed and low, while keeping their heads over their feet and not getting too high or off balance.

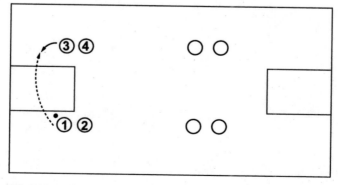

Diagram 21.

Drill 22 — Circle Rebound Drill

Objective:

- To practice blocking out from an "away" position and then rebounding.

Description:

Four players start by moving around the circle — all in the same direction. On the coach's whistle, the two players who are on the bottom of the circle become the defenders blocking out, while the two players on the top of the circle become the offensive players. The two defensive rebounders cross the circle and block out the other two players, getting correct contact position. The coach then tosses the ball in front of them. The closest rebounder releases to the ball, and the other one holds his position. Diagram 22b shows the same drill with the defensive rebounders using a "cross block-out" technique.

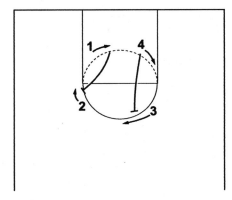

Diagram 22a.

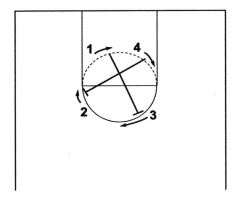

Diagram 22b.

Drill 23 — Ball in the Circle Drill

Objective:

- To practice the "physical" phase of blocking out.

- To teach that blocking out is a team responsibility.

Description:

Four offensive players are positioned around the circle, facing the four defensive players who are on the inside. A ball is placed on the floor in the middle of the circle. On the coach's signal, the defenders pivot and block out the four offensive players, attempting to physically keep them out of the circle and stop them from touching the ball. All players must stay on their feet to avoid collisions. As the defenders get more effective at blocking out, the coach can give the offensive players more freedom to spin, loop, or reverse to get into the circle. The goal of the defense is to keep the offense from getting a hand on the ball for a specified amount of time (e.g., three to five seconds). As players improve, the objective of the activity can become to get three consecutive stops by the defense in order to win the drill.

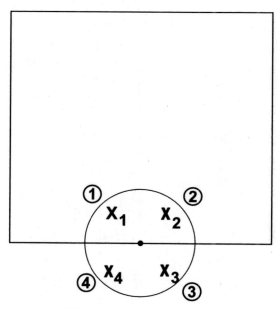

Diagram 23.

Drill 24 — Weave off the Board

Objective:

- To practice lateral footwork and catching the ball at the highest point.

Description:

Three players interchange in a weave replacing each other in a figure eight, while control tipping the ball over the top of the basket. O1 starts with the ball and tips to O3 and follows to O3's side. O3 tips over to O2 and follows to O2's side. O2 tips to O1 and follows, etc. They try to make every controlled tip while they are in the air and successfully continue the drill for at least a minute. The coach can make the drill competitive by using several baskets and seeing which threesome can last the longest.

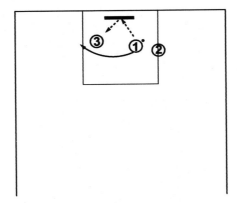

Diagram 24a.

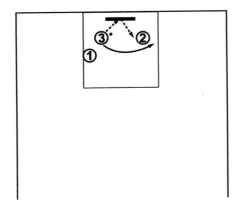

Diagram 24b.

Drill 25 — 3-on-3 Rebounding and Outlet Pass

Objective:

- To practice competitive rebounding.

- To practice the outlet pass.

Description:

Three defensive players are positioned on the inside and attempt to block out the three offensive players. If the defense gets the rebound, they pivot and make an outlet pass to either coach. They get awarded one point, and stay on defense. If the offense gets the rebound without fouling, they get two points and go on defense. The first team to reach 10 points wins. The coaches on the perimeter can pass the ball to each other to shoot, which changes the rebounding angle for the players.

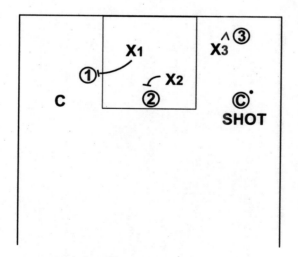

Diagram 25.

Drill 26 — Offensive Rebounding — Leap Frog

Objective:

- To teach players to use both their feet and their arms to move to the inside rebounding position.

Description:

Players get a partner and an assigned space at a basket. One player starts out on the inside position and the other on the outside. On the coach's signal, the outside players use a "step-through" or a spin move to get the inside position. On the next signal, the new outside man uses offensive rebounding techniques to get the inside position. After four exchanges, they move back away from the basket.

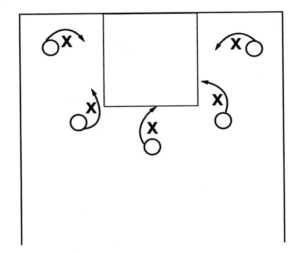

Diagram 26.

Drill 27 – Offensive Rebounding - Cross the Key

Objective:

- To practice offensive rebounding against a zone.

- To practice shooting with defensive pressure.

Description:

The three baseline defenders are stationary and located where they would be in a 2-3 zone. The two offensive players move and cut inside the zone as the coaches move the ball on the perimeter. When one of the coaches shoots the ball, the two offensive players use angle cuts to go across the key to get inside rebounding position. After the inside player rebounds the missed shot, the two closest defenders collapse on him, and he attempts to muscle the ball back up through the defenders, using ball fakes. The coaches can pass the ball to each other to change the rebounding angle of the shot.

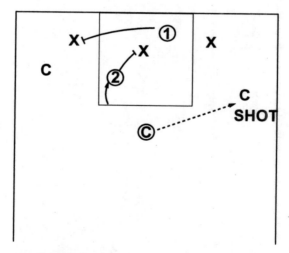

Diagram 27.

CHAPTER 3

DEFENSIVE DRILLS

Drill 28 – Defensive Stance – "Chair"

Objective:

- To practice and reinforce the correct defensive stance.

Description:

The defensive stance is the basis of every defensive skill that will follow. It only takes a few seconds every practice to remind athletes that they need to be able to get into the correct position. Many coaches refer to the defensive stance as being in a "chair". As players come on the floor to practice, you can have a chair in the corner where they enter. Practice begins everyday with each player sitting over the chair in the correct defensive stance, and then sliding off when the coach signals they are in the correct defensive position. This will only take a few seconds and will send the message everyday that the first thing on your list is aggressive defense.

The first thing players should hear as they begin a defensive possession is a verbal cue to all five of them reminding them to get into their stance and get ready to play defense. The key word used to trigger that behavior is "chair." If you want to overemphasize the chair position, you may require players to get into their stance with their heads up when they gather around the coach for group instruction. Staying in their stance for short periods of time (e.g., one-to-two minutes) is also an effective tool for gaining the players' attention during brief instruction periods and can help to strengthen their legs.

Key points for a correct defensive stance:

- The players' feet should be slightly wider than their shoulders and staggered.
- Their knees should be bent, with their hips low to facilitate quick movement in any direction.
- Their body weight should be distributed evenly on the balls of their feet.
- The players' trunks should be slightly forward.
- The players' shoulders should be above their knees, and their heads should be "up".
- Their heads, shoulders and backs should be fairly straight and without much movement.
- Their arms and hands should be in a comfortable position away from their body, but not overextended.
- The hand on the side of their lead foot should be slightly higher with the fingers up, while the other hand should have the palm up.
- When the defenders move, the first thing they move should be their feet, not their hands or upper bodies.
- The defender needs to understand the different stances to use when guarding the ball with a "live dribble", guarding a "dead dribble", and guarding a player off the ball.

Drill 29 – Individual Defense – Close out, Cushion, Ball Up and Ball Down

Objective:

- To practice defensive close outs.
- To practice adjusting the defensive cushion.

Description:

Players choose a partner of approximately the same quickness. They get a basketball and separate about 15–20 feet. On the coach's signal, they one-bounce the ball to their partner. As the ball is in the air, the players passing the ball close out on their partners and assume a defensive stance necessary to guard a live dribble. As the players go from moving forward to getting into a stance, they should take short, choppy steps that make their shoes squeak on the gym floor. The defending players should establish a "cushion", the term for a space between themselves and their partners. This space is based upon the relative quickness between the two. The quicker the defenders are when compared to their partners, the closer the cushion. Conversely, the quicker the dribblers, the more space or cushion the defenders need to give. The cushion will also change depending on the location of the ball. If the offensive players have the ball above their head, the defenders can close their cushions by moving toward their partners. But as the ball is brought down into a position where it can be dribbled, the defenders need to increase their cushions by "crow hopping" back to prevent being beaten on a drive.

The coach's commands are:

- "Close out" – which triggers the pass and a close out by the defenders.
- "Ball up" – which signals the offensive players to move the ball over their heads, allowing the defenders to close their cushions.
- "Ball down" – which signals the offensive players to move the ball down into a working position, forcing the defenders to "crow hop" back.
- "Switch" – which means the defensive players back out to their original 15-20 foot spacing, and the drill can continue with the opposite players closing out.

If you want to add more difficulty, you can have the offensive players take one or more dribbles on command after "ball down", so the defender has to work on his first step (i.e., lead step).

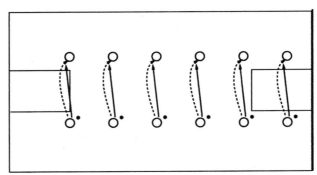

Diagram 29.

Drill 30 — Individual Defense – Zig-Zag

Objective:

- To practice defensive footwork and change of direction while defending the ball.

Description:

Players must stay on one half of the basketball court, which is divided lengthwise. The offensive players begin to dribble at angles until they get to lines on their half of the court, and then they change direction all the way down the court. The defenders keep moving their feet and getting in front of the dribblers at each turn in an attempt to make them change direction.

Different methods of running this drill include:

- The dribblers can be instructed to go about half-speed until the defenders have had success cutting them off.

- At the start of the season, do not let the defenders use their hands. This emphasis will stress playing defense with the feet in order to turn the dribblers.

- Players can take at least one charge as the dribbler changes direction, or try to take as many charges as they can on one trip.

- As the defenders have more success, allow the offensive players to try to beat the defenders. If successful, the offensive players should stop and allow the defenders to start in front again so it isn't a wasted repetition.

- The coach can add a defender (X2) down court to help bluff and slow the dribbler.

- The defender down court can switch if the defender on the ball is beaten.

- Use the middle third of the court as the boundary, and place a help defender on either side to help stop and turn the ball handler.

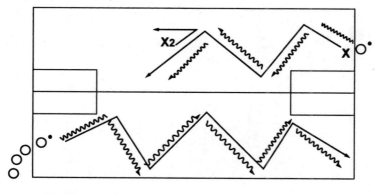

Diagram 30.

Drill 31 — The Basic Eight Drill

Objective:

- To practice eight defensive fundamentals all combined in the same drill.

Description:

This drill is a combination of eight basic defensive skills. It should be introduced as eight individual drills. Once the individual parts of this drill are perfected, the coach can begin to combine them into one continuous drill. Individually, the drills can be practiced in small groups of four or six players and should not take any longer than five minutes apiece. Once the players are able to combine all eight elements of this drill together, it will not take any longer than 30-to-40 seconds per player to go through the entire drill.

The eight phases of this drill are:

- Off the ball (weakside) position.
- Help and recover.
- Close out, ball up, ball down, dead dribble.
- Give and go defense plus clear out.
- Deny to the flash cut.
- Post defensive position (high and low).
- Deny the wing pass and defend the backdoor cut.
- Block out.

Initially, the drill involves taking the individual parts and then combining them into one drill. Diagram 31a shows the coach with the ball and the defender in the drill (X) guarding the weakside offensive player (O).

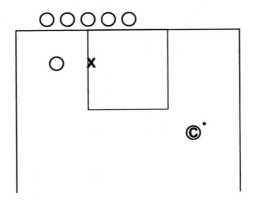

Diagram 31a.

Drill 31: Phase 1 (Situation A) -Weakside Defensive Position – Ball above the line

Objective:

- To practice being in the correct weakside position with the ball above the foul line.

Description:

The coach begins with the ball above the foul-line extended. The defender should be off his man far enough to have one foot in the key and in a stance that allows him to point one hand at the ball and one hand at the offensive player. This "flat triangle" should be deep enough that the defender doesn't have to turn to see either the offensive player or the ball, but flat enough that the offensive player cannot take a direct cut toward the ball without the defender being able to cut him off. The defender should be down in the "chair" position and on his toes with a little bounce.

Drill 31: Phase 1 (Situation B) – Weakside Defensive Position – Ball below the line

Objective:

- To practice adjusting weakside positioning as the ball moves below the foul line.

Description:

The coach dribbles the ball from the beginning position to below the foul-line extended. The defensive player must adjust his position. If the ball is below the line, the weakside defenders should have *both feet* in the key. It is important that the defense gets closer to the ball as the ball gets closer to the basket. The defender still stays in his "flat triangle" stance, pointing his "pistols", one at his man and one at the ball. The coach holds this position until the defender is in the correct position. A second coach can be used to make corrections from behind or next to the individual defender. When weakside position is first taught, it is a good idea to take a long rope and go around the person with the ball, the defender, and the offensive player forming the flat triangle. For players who are visual learners, this step may be all it takes for them to understand the concept of weakside positioning.

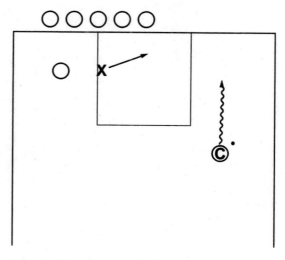

Diagram 31b.

Drill 31: Phase 2 – Help and Recover

Objective:

- To teach the defender to help on the drive from the weak back.

Description:

The defender begins in the flat triangle position with both feet in the key and the ball below the foul-line extended. The coach drives hard to the baseline. The teammates on the baseline call "help". The defender quickly slides over and must meet the coach in a squared-up stance, prepared to take a charge. He must get there, prepared for contact, *outside the key.* If the defender doesn't react quickly enough, the contact will take place inside the key, and, most likely, the referee will call a blocking foul. After the ball has been correctly stopped, the coach dribbles back out, and the defender recovers to his offensive man who has moved to the ball-side elbow.

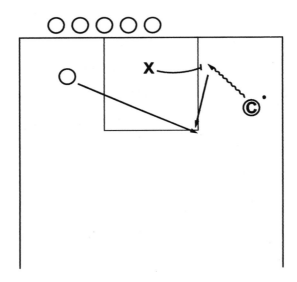

Diagram 31c.

Drill 31: Phase 3 — Close out, ball up, ball down, dead dribble

Objectives:

- To practice closing out on the player with the ball.
- To practice adjusting the cushion.
- To practice defending a dead dribble.

Description:

The defender leaves the coach as the coach backs his dribble out, as if the player who was defending the coach had been able to recover and take that responsibility. The coach bounce passes the ball out to O, and X must close out while standing balanced and under control as discussed in Drill 29. The offensive player then works on making the defender adjust his cushion (Drill 29) by bringing the ball up and holding it for a two-second count and then bringing the ball down in a dribbling position, forcing the defender to "crow hop" back (ball up, ball down). The offensive player then dribbles the ball back and picks it up at about the top of the circle. At this point, the defender goes from checking a live dribble to checking a *dead dribble*. The defender closes his cushion down tight, traces the ball with both hands, and calls "dead, dead, dead". This signal alerts the other defenders that they can concentrate more on denying their man the ball and less on helping.

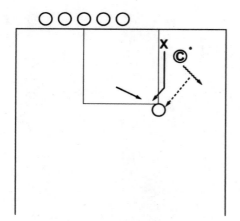

Diagram 31d.

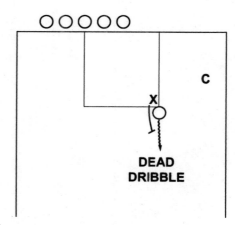

Diagram 31e.

Drill 31: Phase 4 — Defending the Give-and-Go and the Clear Out

Objective:

- To practice the technique required to defend a "give-and-go" cut.

- To practice the technique required to defend a clear out.

Description:

The coach has moved back out to the wing, and after the defender has correctly traced the dead dribble, the offensive player passes the ball to the coach. After passing the ball, the offensive player "V" cuts away for a step and then makes a direct cut to the basket (give-and-go). After getting to the low block, he cuts away and clears out to the weakside of the court.

The defender who is checking a dead dribble must "jump to the ball" as soon as the offensive player passes the ball to the coach. He jumps far enough toward the ball so that the offensive player cannot make a cut on the "ball-side" of him. As the cutter begins to go to the basket, X must keep a "shoulder-to-shoulder" relationship with him. The defender's inside shoulder needs to be even with the outside shoulder of the cutter so that the defender can deny any return pass from the coach. This period is a critical time for the defender; he cannot relax as his offensive man passes the ball, thinking his job is finished. The defender has to immediately jump in the direction of the pass and get into a denial stance. As the offensive player cuts through the key to the weakside, the defender gets back into the correct weakside flat triangle position, based upon the location of his man and the ball.

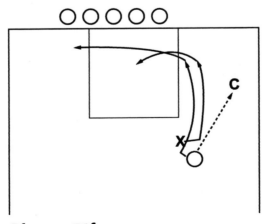

Diagram 31f.

Drill 31: Phase 5 – Deny the Flash Cut

Objective:

- To practice defending the flash cut.

Description:

This phase begins with the offensive player having cleared out to the weakside, and the coach with the ball on the foul-line extended. The defender has stayed in the key as his man cleared to the weakside and is in a "flat-triangle", "pistols" position. As the coach slaps the ball, the offensive player jab steps and makes a "flash cut" to the elbow. The defender jumps up into the line between his man and the ball to deny the direct pass. The defender gets his top hand and foot in the passing lane and lets the cushion gradually decrease until there is physical contact with his bottom forearm on the cutters chest. He doesn't try to halt the cutter's progress; he just attempts to get the cutter to slow down, change his path, and not be able to receive a direct pass from the coach.

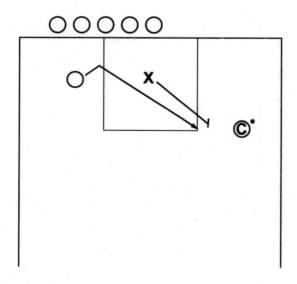

Diagram 31g.

Drill 31: Phase 6 – Defending the High Post and the Low Post Positions

Objectives:

- To practice the techniques necessary to defend a player at the high post.
- To practice the techniques necessary to defend a player in the low post.

Description:

After the defender has jammed the flash cut, he must beat the cutter to the spot the cutter is going to. The offensive player attempts to get as close to the elbow as he can on his cut so the defensive position on the high post can be evaluated. The defender should be ahead of the cutter when he gets to the high post. The defender verbalizes "HIGH POST" and then makes sure that his top hand and foot are between the ball and his man. His back foot is below the high post, and his back hand is behind him so he can feel if the high post player is going to release to the basket.

After the defender has successfully beaten the offinsive player to the high post, the offensive player holds for a two-count and then slides down the lane to the low-post position. The defender drops, using the same technique he did to defend the give-and-go (i.e., shoulder-to- shoulder drop). Once the offensive player gets to the low post, he again holds that position while the coach checks the defenders low-post technique. If you want the low post offensive player "fronted", the defender gets his feet, hands, and body in front of the post player and calls "FRONT". If you want to play behind or on the side of the post player, your defender gets to that position and calls "BACK". Since the defensive rotation by the other defensive players depends on whether the post defender you are playing is in front or behind the offensive player in the low post, it is essential that your defender verbalizes his position as either in front or behind. If you are not familiar with proper team defensive rotation, please refer to my video on *Individual and Team Defense* (see the About the Author section).

After the player has successfully defended the low post, the coach throws a skip pass across court to a second coach or player. The offensive player at the post holds his position, while the defender gets over the top of him and into the correct weakside position (Diagram 31i).

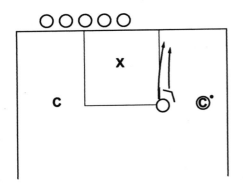

Diagram 31h.

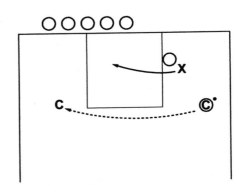

Diagram 31i.

Drill 31: Phase 7 – Deny the Wing Pass and Defend the Backdoor Cut

Objectives:

- To practice the techniques necessary to deny the direct pass to the wing.

- To practice the techniques necessary to defend the back-door cut.

Description:

The action continues with the defender in a weakside position, and the ball at the foul-line extended. The offensive player cuts toward the ballside wing and out to the three-point line. The defender denies his initial cut across the key by being in front, and then steps on top of the cutter as he starts to pop out to the wing. His top hand and foot are up in the passing lane as he denies the cut to the three-point line. His top hand is open, and his thumb is down to form a "stop sign" to the passer. He continues to work hard to move his feet and deny the ball to his man, as the offensive player makes three cuts to the perimeter. He cannot allow his opponent to catch the ball inside the three-point line, and wants him to be going away from the basket if he does catch it. The coach doesn't pass the ball to the cutter unless he is open inside the three-point line. After his third cut to the perimeter, the offensive player makes a hard, back-cut to the basket. Depending on which method you teach, the defender must either correctly open to the ball or swivel his head to deny the pass to the back-door cutter.

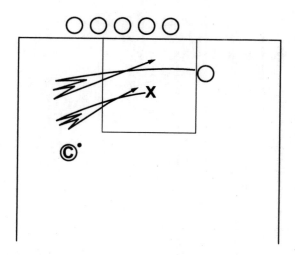

Diagram 31j.

Drill 31: Phase 8 – Block Out

Objective:

- To practice block-out technique from the weakside.

Description:

After the offensive player has taken a backdoor cut, he clears out to the weakside. The coach waits until he clears, and then he shoots the ball. The defender must leave his help position, off the ball, and go block out the offensive player.

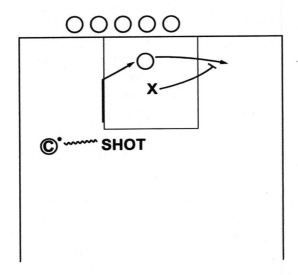

Diagram 31k.

The foregoing completes the eight different phases of the **Basic Eight Drill.** Once the individual phases of this drill have been taught, drilled, and correctly executed by the team members, the next three pages explain how to combine these eight phases into a single drill and to add difficulty to the drill.

Adding Difficulty to the Basic Eight Drill

The first thing a coach should do after working on the eight phases of this drill separately is to gradually add the various components of this drill together. For example, combine just the first two phases of the drill together (off-the-ball position and help and recover). Then, continue to combine different phases without stopping in between (e.g., give-and-go, clear out, flash post, and post-defensive position). Eventually, you probably will want to run the entire eight phases of the drill without stopping.

Once you have your players able to understand and execute the eight phases correctly without stopping, the drill can be made more difficult by:

- Gradually increasing the speed of the offensive man.

- Having the players only go as far as they can before they make a mistake. Once they make an error, have them stop the drill, go to a side coach and explain what they did incorrectly to the coach. This step is not a punishment, but rather an opportunity for the coach to see if the players really understand the techniques and have just made a physical error. If they don't understand the techniques, it provides a chance for the coach to make corrections. You will be amazed by how hard your players will try to get through the whole drill without making a mistake. Work on perfection!

- Stopping them on the slightest error, once you know they can successfully do the drill (e.g., not having their hands in the "pistols" position or not being low enough in their stance).

- Giving them one chance everyday (e.g., one at the beginning of practice or one toward the end) to perform the drill. This puts more importance on the attempts they get. Be willing to stay after practice to help them understand what they did wrong, and how they can be successful the following day.

- Having the players who make an error immediately go to the side coach for individual correction instead of stopping the drill and having everyone wait while each player is corrected. Once the players' ability to perform the drill has reached a competitive level, each player should be able to get through the eight phases in about 15 to 20 seconds, allowing you to get your entire squad through the drill in less than six to eight minutes.

- To increase the length of the drill, refer to Diagram 31L. This is the phase where you would normally shoot the ball for the defender to block out. Instead, you could start the drill completely over again, but from the opposite side. The defender is in the weakside position with the ball above the foul-line extended (phase #1). The coach could go right into ball-below-the-line, help-and-recover, etc. The entire drill performed at full speed on both sides usually takes less than 45 seconds per player.

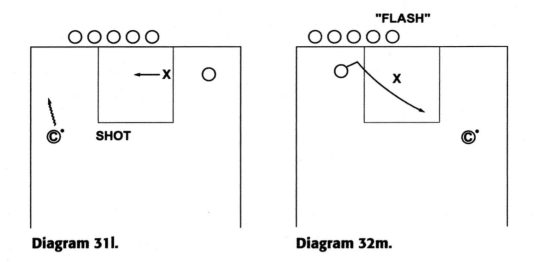

Diagram 31l.   **Diagram 32m.**

Methods to Improve the Quality of the Basic Eight Drill

- Have your players who are waiting on the baseline help the player in the drill by making the defensive calls with him. This step will carry over into 5-on-5 defense and improve your team's defensive talk.

    - Phase 1: Remind the defensive player to get in his stance by calling "CHAIR".

    - Phase 2: Call "HELP" when the coach drives.

    - Phase 3: Call "DEAD" when the offensive player picks up the dribble.

    - Phase 4: Call "JUMP" as the ball is passed and the offensive player starts his give- and-go cut.

    - Phase 5: Call "FLASH" as the cutter moves toward the high post.

    - Phase 6: Call "FRONT" or "BACK" depending how the defender is playing the low post.

    - Phase 7: Call "DENY" as he denies the wing pass and "OPEN" as he opens up to deny the backdoor cut.

    - Phase 8: Call "SHOT" as the coach shoots to trigger the block-out action.

- Set a goal for your team to have each player to make it through the whole drill without making a mistake sometime during the season.

- Set a goal for them all to make it through on the same day without a mistake.

- Explain to the players that this drill is more difficult than any 20 seconds of defense they will encounter in a game, and because they are the only person "on stage", they are open to closer inspection and correction than they will ever be with five defenders on the floor.

- Have one or two players (managers) learn the pattern of the offensive man (Diagrams 31n and 31o). The better they can run the pattern, the easier it will be for you to require perfect execution by the defender.

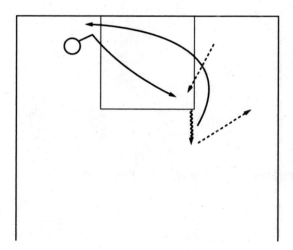

Diagram 31n.

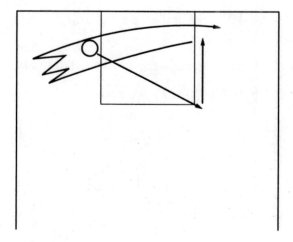

Diagram 31o.

Drill 32 — Team Defense — 4-on-4 Close Outs

Objective:

- To practice correct close-out position based on the location of the ball.

Description:

Four offensive players stand on the perimeter, while the four defenders begin on the baseline with the coach. As the ball is passed on one bounce to any one of the perimeter players, all four defenders close out as quickly as possible to the proper position. Their position is based upon whether they are on the strongside or on the weakside, and if the ball is above or below the foul line.

Once the defenders have closed out into the correct defensive position and stance, the coach signals, and they hustle back to the baseline and prepare for the next close out. Have the players rotate from waiting out to defense, from defense to offense, and from offense to waiting out. After this phase has been taught correctly, and you are just trying to get some quality repetitions, the whole team should be able to rotate through this drill in a maximum of about three-to-four minutes. You can have each player waiting in line be responsible for the corrections of the man in front of him, along with the coach who watches all four players.

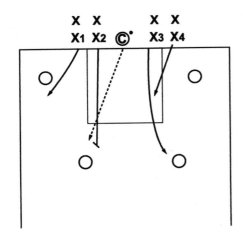

Diagram 32a.

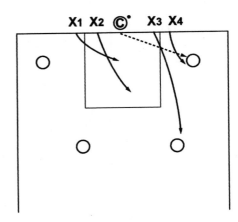

Diagram 32b.

Drill 33 — Team Defense — 4-on-4 Close Outs with Added Difficulty

Objective:

- To add difficulty and additional techniques to the 4-on-4 close out drill.

Description:

The coach can build on the previous drill in the following ways:

1. Ball up, ball down — As the players close out on the ball, the player who receives the ball works his defender by raising the ball up and down to make the defender change his cushion.

2. Ball up, ball down, one dribble — This option adds the lead step for the "on-the-ball defender", and as soon as the offensive player picks up his dribble, it creates a dead dribble situation for all the other defenders.

3. Help and recover (Diagram 33a) — Allow the player receiving the pass to try to penetrate one of the gaps in the defense. All other defenders must adjust their positions and be ready to help until the penetration is stopped.

4. Weakside exchange (Diagram 33b) — As the ball is passed to one side of the floor, the two weakside offensive players exchange from top-to-bottom. This procedure causes the two defenders on that side to correctly slide through to their new positions.

5. Weakside screen (Diagram 33c) — As the ball is caught on one side of the floor, the two weakside offensive players set either a down screen or a back screen. This provides an opportunity for those two defenders to work on correctly defending those screens.

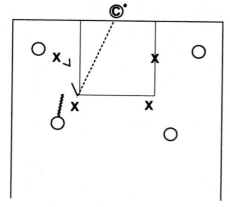

Diagram 33a.

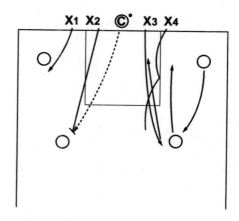

Diagram 33b.

6. Add a pass on the perimeter (Diagram 33d) – As the first pass is caught from the coach, that offensive player holds the ball until all four defenders are in the proper positions, and then makes another pass. He can pass to any of the other three offensive players. The defenders allow the pass to get through and jump to their new positions based upon the location of the ball and their man. A good defender will get relocated during the flight time of the pass, so that he is already in the correct spot as the ball is caught.

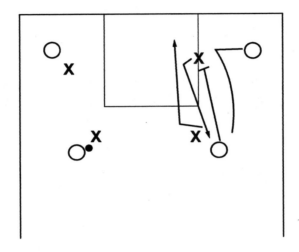

Diagram 33c.

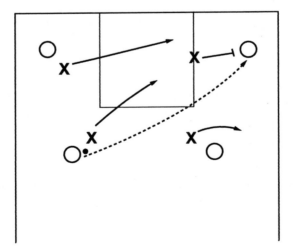

Diagram 33d.

Variety can be added to this drill by playing 4-on-4 half-court with the offensive team having two additional players (managers) located in the corners, so the four defenders are responsible for stopping six offensive players. The two offensive players in the corner can receive a pass at anytime, and upon reception, can immediately drive the ball to the basket. The four defenders are matched up and playing man-to-man on the four offensive players who are stationary to begin the drill. The defense cannot intercept any passes on the perimeter and should be ready to help and rotate to stop any of the drives by the corner players.

The following adjustments can be made to add difficulty to this drill:

- Make the defenders play with their hands behind their backs or with a towel behind their backs.

- Allow the offensive players to dribble penetrate, forcing the defense to help and recover, as well as win their battle on the ball.

- Allow the offensive players to exchange.

- Allow the offensive players to screen.

- Allow the offensive players to post up.

- Eliminate all restrictions on the offense.

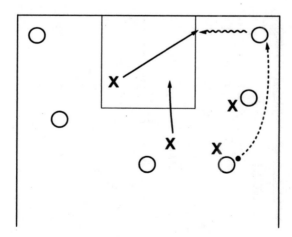

Diagram 33e.

Drill 34 — Team Defense — 4-on-4 Three Stops

Objective:

• To practice four-on-four team defense in various competitive situations.

Description:

This exercise is a competitive drill that requires all four defenders to successfully defend in the half-court three consecutive times. Divide your squad into three or more teams of four players each. Team A is on defense against team B, while team C waits at half-court. Team A stays on defense until they get three team stops in a row.

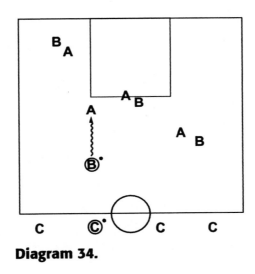

Diagram 34.

Team A must get a successful "stop" on team B in order to have it count. A successful stop could be anything the coach decides to call it, from very simple to more demanding. Examples of what could be defined as a defensive "stop" include:

• The offense doesn't score.

• The offense doesn't score or get an offensive rebound.

• The offense doesn't score, get an offensive rebound, or get an "uncontested" shot.

• The offense doesn't score, get an offensive rebound, or a shot in the key, etc.

The next offensive team has their own ball and is ready to come on as soon as the defensive team wins or loses their stop. The next team does not have to wait until the defense is ready. As soon as the previous offensive team clears the court, the next offensive team is coming right at the defense. This forces the defense to quickly recover from the last stop and match up with the new players. The coach identifies and counts the stops. A loss puts the defensive team back at zero.

Drill 35 — Team Defense — 4-on-4 Perfection

Objective:

- To provide a quick moving, competitive defensive game.

- To provide an opportunity for coaches to identify individual mistakes.

Description:

In order to run this drill, your players need to be able to:

- Take correction as a compliment.

- Accept the coaches' judgement.

- Understand that the coach is trying to help them, by identifying their defensive mistakes.

- Accept the judgment and quickly move in and out of the drill.

In this drill, four players are on offense, four on defense and four are waiting in order to enter the game on defense. The coach stands where he has the best vision and stops the game *anytime* he sees a defensive error by an individual or group. On the coach's whistle, the game is stopped, the mistake is quickly pointed out, that defensive player(s) goes to the end of the line under the basket, and the first player in line replaces him on defense. The offensive team immediately goes on the attack until the next whistle. The four players that are on offense, stay on offense for three minutes, and at the end of the period and during the next correction, the coach calls "change". At that time, the four players waiting in line go to offense and the offensive players get in line to rotate in on defense.

Because the coach will not have time to discuss each defensive error in depth, he should simply identify it and get on with the drill. The head coach may want to have a second coach on the sideline to talk to the eliminated player about the defensive mistake.

It will help your players if you can identify the specific defensive mistakes that you notice and then work on eliminating them. Among the more commonly made defensive mistakes are the following:

- A player is not in a good defensive stance.

- A player is out of position.

- A player does not verbalize — *"shot, help, screen, front, back, switch"* or any other verbal cues that are required on defense.

- A player is beaten on a drive or requires help.

- A player misses block outs.

- A player does not contest a shot.

- A player does not play a screen correctly.

- A player trails a cutter.

The aforementioned are just a few examples of the factors that could cause a player to go to the end of the line and have to wait to get back in on defense. The coach may want to take just one or two of these errors and have them be his "emphasis of the day" and only substitute for those errors. The goal of each player should be to stay in on defense for as long as possible. This drill can be done for three rotations (nine minutes).

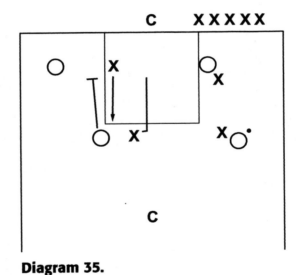

Diagram 35.

Drill 36 — Team Defense — Deny the Flash, Stop the Drive

Objectives:

- To combine and practice the defensive techniques involved in denying the flash post.

- To practice stopping the drive at game speed.

Description:

Two offensive players begin at the top of the three-point line, each with a basketball. Two offensive players are on the wings without a ball. One defender is in the middle of the circle. The coach stands behind the defender and out of his vision. The primary purposes of this drill are:

- To improve defensive vision.

- Deny the flash cut.

- Be able to stop dribble penetration.

The single defender must be ready to check any of the four offensive players. If the coach points at one of the offensive players on the wing, he flashes into the high post area (Diagram 36a). The defender must jam his cut and beat him to the spot. If the defender is successful, the offensive player retreats back to his original spot.

If the coach points at either of the two top offensive players with the basketballs, they drive to the basket (Diagram 36b). The defender must stop their penetration and flatten them out to be successful. If the defender is successful, the dribbler retreats back to his starting position. After the players have learned the drill, each player can go about 30 – 45 seconds.

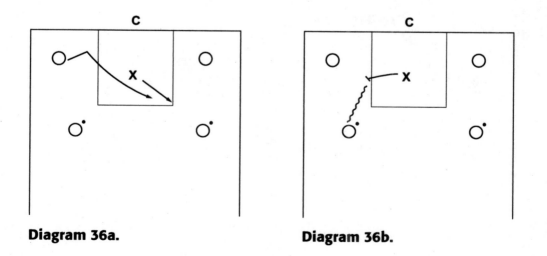

Diagram 36a.   **Diagram 36b.**

Drill 37 – Team Defense – 5-on-5 Change

Objectives:

- To improve defensive transition.
- To work on getting matched up quickly.
- To work on stopping the ball.
- To enhance communication between defenders.
- To improve endurance and stamina.

Description:

Five defensive players are matched up with five offensive players at one end of the court. The five offensive players are moving and screening without any restrictions. On the coach's whistle, any offensive player who has the ball simply places it on the floor, and the offensive team converts to the defensive end of the floor. The team that was on defense picks up the ball and converts to offense.

The team dropping back to defense must match up with a different player than the one that was checking them. In order to do this, they must quickly turn and face the oncoming team and verbalize who they are going to check. It is essential that the first person to match up takes the ball and attempts to stop any penetration.

As soon as the coach wants the players to transition to the other end, he simply blows his whistle, and the ball gets placed on the floor. At this point, the new defensive team must locate and match up with different people. Five-to-eight minutes will give your team several transitions.

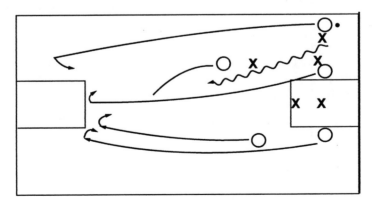

Diagram 37.

CHAPTER 4

AGGRESSIVENESS DRILLS

Overview

Before you begin to demand aggressiveness out of your players, it is essential that you understand the emotional, physical and psychological development of the age group with which you are working. Some players are naturally aggressive, while others have never been asked to be, but are capable of learning to be aggressive. There also is that group of players who do not have it in their personalities to ever be aggressive. The coach must match the needs of the athletes with his own expectations for aggressiveness and use good judgement in his choice of drills.

It is also important to match up players of equal strength and quickness when performing any drills to promote aggressiveness. Most individual- and team-level aggressiveness can be improved simply by verbally reinforcing any action that could be deemed aggressive for that individual player.

Drill 38 — Aggressiveness - Rip Away

Objective:

- To practice having players gain possession in tie-up situations.

Description:

This drill requires two players working together with one basketball. Both players begin with one hand on the basketball, holding it between them. Their other hand is in contact with their side. On the coach's whistle, they can use their second hand to try to gain possession of the ball. The coach should only allow them about three seconds to gain control of the ball so that they do not end up wrestling on the floor. The rules of basketball allow a player one tug when joint possession occurs. For younger or weaker players, the skill of quickly and aggressively pulling the ball toward themselves can help avoid a lot of jump-ball calls.

For younger players, you can start with both hands on the ball. To add more aggressiveness to the drill, the coach can allow the player who gains possession to "chin" the ball and pivot, while the partner attempts to slap the ball from his hands. The player trying to slap the ball should try to move around in front and not reach over or around the player with the ball. The player who is pivoting should protect the ball with strong hands, his elbows should be out, and he should pivot to keep his opponent behind him.

Drill 39 — Aggressiveness – Snake Drill

Objective:

- To practice hand quickness and aggressiveness in recovering a loose ball.

Description:

This drill involves a slightly higher level of agressiveness than the previous drill. It will help your players learn how to gain possession of the basketball without being tied up for a jump ball. The two players stand facing each other, and a third player with the basketball stands so that he can hold the ball out directly between them. Without any warning, the third player drops the ball between the two players who are attempting to gain possession (somewhat like a hockey face off). The two players attempting to gain possession must allow the ball to hit the ground twice before they can go after it. This element gets them low to the ground, so they can pick it up quickly after it hits the floor for the second time. The player who has the quickest hands and can react to the second bounce will have an advantage. Once one of the players has gained control, he should quickly and aggressively pivot away from the second player to avoid being tied up.

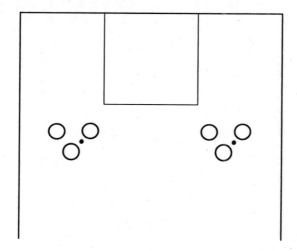

Diagram 39.

To add a little bit more difficulty to the previous drill, group the players in teams of three with one basketball. Have the players select their group based upon comparable height or jumping ability. The third player tosses the ball up between the two other players who are trying to gain possession. They attempt to shield each other off from the ball, so that when one of them gets possession, they have their opponent on their back. This teaches them how to go after the ball, while at the same time, how to turn their bodies to make their opponents have to come over their backs to get a hand on the ball. It also encourages getting the ball at the highest point after establishing position.

To make the drill even slightly more difficult, the player tossing the ball can throw it out four-to-eight feet away from the two players instead of directly above them. This action gives the advantage to the player who blocks out and then moves his feet under the ball. The coach can make the requirement that the ball must bounce once on the floor to encourage the players to hold the block-out position longer.

Drill 40 — Aggressiveness – Toss and Go for the Basket

Objectives:

- To practice recovering a loose ball.

- To practice taking the ball aggressively to the basket against pressure.

Description:

The coach stands with a basketball between two lines of players. The first player in each line prepares to go after the ball. The further you have the two lines go to get to the basketball, the more speed they will build up, and the more aggressive this drill can become. Begin with the lines five or six feet apart, positioned on the three-point line facing the basket. Gradually allow them to go for the ball from a greater distance, while still maintaining safety.

Once one of the players has gained possession, he becomes the offensive player. He keeps the defender on his back protecting the ball, and takes it strong to the basket, while concentrating on "playing through the contact". *Do not allow your defender to foul or go up with the shooter, but encourage him to strip the ball off the dribble, or cross in front of the shooter.*

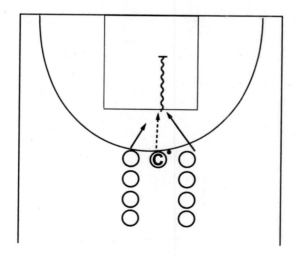

Diagram 40.

Drill 41 — Aggressiveness – Blocking Dummies

Objective:

- To practice to taking the ball strong to the basket and score while being fouled.

Description:

The coach needs to borrow two blocking dummies or blocking shields from a football coach and use them to help prepare his players to shoot while being fouled or bumped. The coach can begin this drill by having one of his players toss a ball off the backboard and rebound his own toss. Then, the player takes the ball back up to the basket, while the two coaches with blocking shields bump or jostle him in order try to to knock him off balance. The player keeps following his shot until it goes in. Next, the coach moves the players back from the basket and has them catch a pass on the way to the basket and take it up between the two coaches with blocking shields. Coaches should give them enough contact to force them to concentrate and be strong with the ball, but still allow them have a chance to make their shots.

Practice having players approach the basket from different angles and distances. Set the drill up so that they are having to use their weak hand to lay the ball in, or give them contact before they get into the key to teach them how to dribble through traffic and then clear themselves to the basket. Players who can play through being fouled or bumped will learn to maintain their poise and skills and not have to wait for the referee to save them when games get physical.

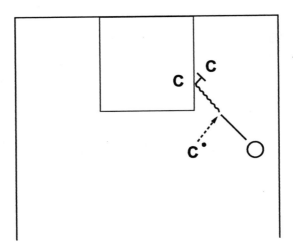

Diagram 41.

Drill 42 — Aggressiveness – Block Out of the Circle

Objective:

- To practice the physical part of blocking out.

Description:

Two players stand back to back in the center of the circle. The primary goal of the drill is simple — players need to keep contact and attempt to drive the other person's feet out of the circle. As soon as one player's feet touch the circle, they lose. This drill teaches your players to keep their weight on the balls of their feet, and their shoulders and back on their opponent as they are blocking out.

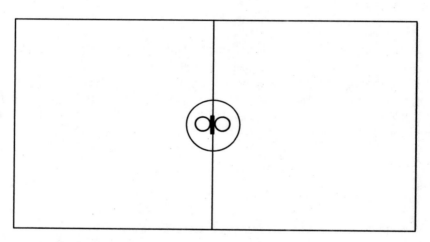

Diagram 42.

Drill 43 — Aggressiveness – Bull in the Ring

Objectives:

- To practice aggressively attempting to get open.
- To practice defending in the post area.

Description:

The coach divides the squad into two teams with each player having a partner on the opposite team who is about the same size. Two people (A1 and B1) at a time go into the post with one on defense and one on offense. If A1 goes on offense first, his four teammates become the perimeter passers on the three-point line.

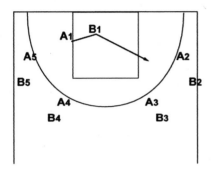   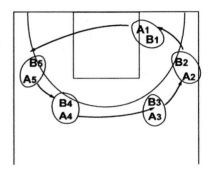

Diagram 43a.   **Diagram 43b.**

The perimeter players have one basketball. They attempt to get the ball to A1 as many times as possible in 30 seconds. In order for a pass to count as a reception in the post, A1 must have at least one foot in the key when he catches the ball. The members of the "A" team on the perimeter can pass the ball directly into A1 or pass it around the perimeter to attempt to get a better passing angle into the post. It will also count as a reception if the defense obviously fouls the receiver. It is the coach's judgement what constitutes a foul.

As soon as A1 catches the ball in the post, he passes it directly out to any of his teammates on the perimeter. He is not limited in his movement within the key and can get multiple passes from the same player. When A1 has gone 30 seconds, B1 enters the ring and is checked by A1. The "B" team members, who have been waiting on the perimeter, now replace the "A" perimeter players and try to get as many post-entry passes as possible into B1. When both players have had their turn in the post, the teams rotate, and it becomes B2 on offense against A2 (Diagram 43b). It is important to alternate which team goes first in the post, because of how much energy is expended on defending the post.

The coach should continue to rotate the team members until all players have been on offense and defense in the post. The team with the most total receptions in the post, wins. This drill also helps the perimeter players improve their post-passing skills.

Drill 44 — Aggressiveness – Blood and Guts

Objective:

- To practice continuing to play through fouls.

Description:

Three players move in to the key area and prepare for the coach to shoot. The coach starts at the foul line and shoots the ball, attempting to miss. All three players are on offense until the ball is controlled by one of the players. As soon as one player gets the ball, he attempts to score. The two players without the ball immediately convert to defense and try to stop the third player from scoring. They can hold, push, and foul the player with the ball as long as it does not endanger him. As soon as the ball is shot, the drill continues with all three players going after the ball, whether it is made or missed, and then attempting to score against the other two players. The first player to score three baskets wins. Players will learn to battle for the rebounds and to not stop playing when they are fouled.

If the coach would like to make this into a team drill, he can divide the team up into four teams of three players each and arrange them from the tallest to the shortest. The first person representing each team is their tallest player, the second is their next tallest, etc. The team with the most total baskets after every player has gone through the drill is the winner.

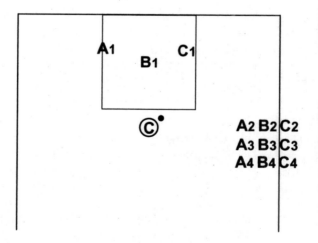

Diagram 44.

Drill 45 — Aggressiveness – Scramble

Objective:

- To practice and reward aggressiveness when going after a loose ball.

Description:

The coach lines up five players on the baseline and places four basketballs on the foul line. On the whistle, the five players scramble for the four basketballs. Once the four players have picked up the four balls, they must dribble into front court and continue to dribble.

The one player who did not get a ball attempts to take a ball away from any of the four other players. He has 30 seconds to try to steal a ball from one of the dribblers. At the end of 30 seconds, the player without a basketball is eliminated.

To make the drill more difficult, the coach can continue eliminating players by then only putting three basketballs on the foul line and having the four players who survived the last round on the baseline go for the basketballs. He can keep going until there are only two players and one basketball remaining.

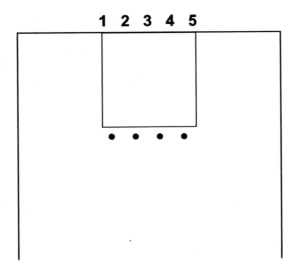

Diagram 45.

CHAPTER 5

FAST BREAK DRILLS

Overview

How a coach decides to drill for a fast break, depends on his offensive philosophy. If you are a "patterned" or "numbered" fast break team, your drills will focus on rehearsing the cuts and reads that your players will have to execute, based on their prearranged positions on the floor. If your offense only fast breaks when there is a defensive turnover or long rebound then you should spend the majority of your fast break time on "turnover"-type fast break drills. If you are a scrambling, pressing-type team that requires all of your players to be ball handlers, decision-makers, and finishers, then your drills need to reflect those situations and the skills needed to be successful.

In general, only four phases of the fast break exist that drills must be designed to duplicate (Refer to Table 5.1). By looking at your overall fast-breaking philosophy and focusing on these four areas, a coach can identify which fast break drills will be useful to his team.

Table 5.1 – The four phases of the fast break.

• The defensive rebound and outlet pass.
• The transition down the floor in order to outnumber or out position the defense.
• The decision making process by the passer(s).
• The catching, shooting and offensive rebounding completion of the break.

Drill 45 — Rebound, Outlet, Run and Finish

Objective:

- To provide repetitions for the rebounding, decision-making, and finishing parts of the fast break.

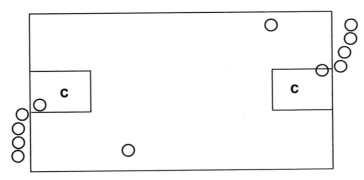

Diagram 45a.

Description:

The coaches stand in the lane on either end of the floor and hold the blocking shields. They pressure the rebounder with the shield as he rebounds the ball off the board and then bump the finisher as he catches the ball from the guard.

The rebounder tosses the ball off the board and goes up to get it. He makes a quarter turn to the outside while in the air to keep the coach with the blocking shield on his back. He outlets the ball to the guard and sprints to the outside of the court until he gets ahead of the ball. Once he gets to the foul-line extended, he comes under control, shows his hands, and angle cuts toward the basket. As he catches the ball with both hands, he reads the coach with the shield. If the coach is squared up with him ready to take a charge, he stops and takes the short jump shot. If the coach has given him a driving lane, he takes the ball strong to the basket, through the contact by the blocking shield.

The outlet man starts on the elbow and sprints to the designated (taped) area of the floor where the coach wants the outlet pass received. The outlet man has his back toward the sideline and calls for the ball. As soon as he receives the pass, he gets his *"eyes up court"*, and pushes the ball toward the center of the court with a speed dribble. As the dribbler crosses through the center circle, he brings his speed under control and "settles" to make the pass. The player makes an easy decision and attempts to put the ball directly into the cutter's hands so that he can finish.

The finisher gets the ball and goes to the rebounding line under the basket, and the guard goes to the next outlet line after making the pass. For the sake of safety, the rebounders waiting on the baseline should be out of the way of the finishers, and the guards pushing the ball down the court should stay on the their half of the court.

Based upon the age and ability of your athletes, this drill can be broken down into three separate drills:

- The rebound and outside pivot (Diagram 45b).
- The outlet pass and push by the rebounder and guard (Diagram 45c).
- Just the finishing end of the drill with the guard and cutter starting at half-court and finishing against the coach with the hand shield. (Diagram 45d).

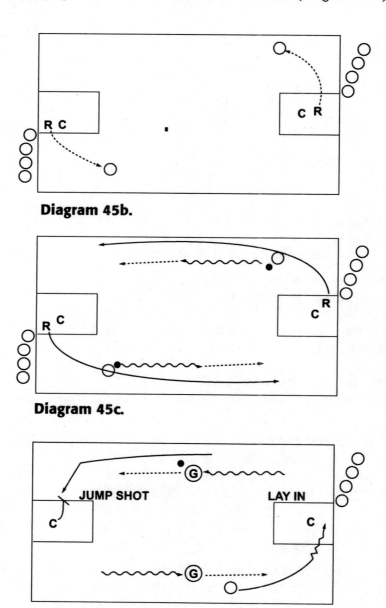

Diagram 45b.

Diagram 45c.

Diagram 45d.

Drill 46 — Outlet, Long Pass and Finish

Objectives:

- To teach the guards to make the *long sideline pass.*

- To teach the receivers proper *take off, catch and finish.*

Description:

This drill is set up similar to the previous drill, except the rebounder does not run the court. As the rebounder tosses the ball off the backboard, O2 takes off like a sprinter as soon as he can see that the rebounder is going to gain possession. He widens and sprints at half-court, he checks over his inside shoulder and at the two-thirds point down the court, he breaks out of the sprint and glides under control as he catches the ball. O2 attempts to finish aggressively against the hand shield of the coach. If O2 has a tendency to leave early, a coach could toss the ball off the board in such a way that makes O2 have to wait and see if the rebounder will get it or the coach will get it. The coach can also have the rebounders waiting on the baseline call "now" when they are sure the ball will be rebounded by his teammate. After rebounding and outleting the ball, the rebounders rotate to the position that O2 had played, where they *sprint, catch and finish.*

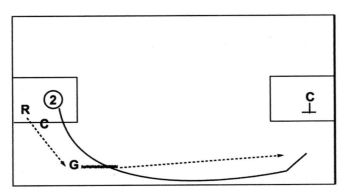

Diagram 46.

The outlet man gets to the designated outlet area and calls for the ball. As soon as he receives the ball, he gets his eyes up court and attempts to "throw a rope" to O2 cutting hard down his sideline. With younger players, find the distance that they can successfully throw this pass and gradually try to increase the distance. Younger players can take a dribble or two to shorten the distance if they do not have enough strength to make this pass from the outlet spot. This drill can be run on both sides of the court at the same time, alternating which side of the court is going.

Drill 47 — 3-on-2 From Half Court

Objectives:

- To practice decision making and finishing.
- To practice offensive rebounding.

Description:

This drill helps players in a decision-making role make quick, yet easy decisions. One player is always open, and players do *not* need three or four passes to get an easy shot. Offensive players are also rebounding 3-on-2, so if the first shot is missed, there is no excuse for not getting a second shot. The coach can keep the same two defensive men for several rotations and then switch them both.

The offensive wing players come down the court wide, carrying both hands above their elbows with their fingers spread, giving the passer a target. The appropriate term in this situation is "target the ball". The decision-maker needs to make a quick decision as he gets into the attack area of the floor. He needs to make the simplest play that is going to get his team a shot. The decision-maker needs to avoid trying to make the "great pass" that might get his team a shot but might cause a turnover. The worst thing that can happen for the offensive team is to not get a shot when they have a 3-on-2 advantage. Not getting a shot also does not give the offensive team an opportunity for a rebound. Part of the decision-making process is to know your teammates' strengths and weaknesses. The player who is making the decisions with the basketball needs to know the abilities of the players on either side of him. If he has a "shooter" on one side and a non-shooting, rebounder on the other, he must play to their relative strengths by letting the shooter shoot and the rebounder rebound.

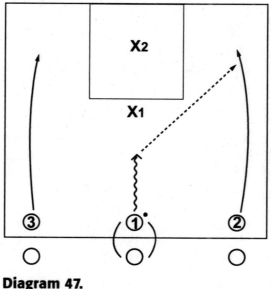

Diagram 47.

Drill 48 — 3-on-2 With a Chaser

Objectives:

- To practice quick decision making and attacking offensively when having a numerical advantage.

- To add realism to a 3-on-2 situation.

Description:

This drill begins with all three offensive players on the half-court line. Two defenders are waiting in the key, and the third defender starts at the far foul line. As soon as the coach calls "go", the offense can attack, and the third defender sprints to help. This is a good defensive transition drill as well, with the two defenders trying to hold off the offense until the third defender can get there. When the third defender arrives, all three defenders must verbally communicate to effectively match up. The three offensive players must make a quick decision if they are to get a shot against the two defenders. If for some reason, they do not get a good shot before the third defender arrives, they simply play 3-on-3 using their offensive rules.

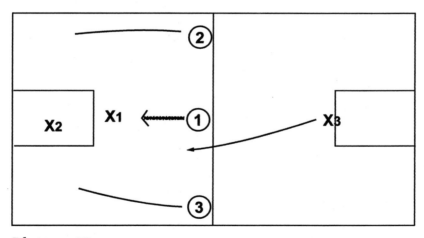

Diagram 48.

Drill 49 — 3-on-2 — 2-on-1

Objectives:

- To practice offensive decision-making and finishing when a numerical advantage exists.

- To practice defending the basket when there is a numerical disadvantage.

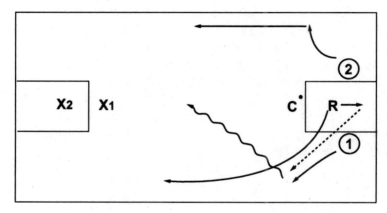

Diagram 49a.

Description:

This drill begins with the coach having the ball at the foul line. The rebounder is under the basket, and the two outlet men are on the elbows. As the shot goes up, the rebounder goes after it using the techniques described earlier, and the two outlet men get to their designated spots. The rebounder outlets the ball and sprints to that same sideline. The guard who receives the pass pushes the ball hard to the middle of the floor as the third player fills the other lane. They attack two defenders (X1 and X2) trying to get a "good" shot (Diagram 49a).

As soon as the defense gets the ball on a rebound, a made shot, or a turnover, the two defenders go on offense to the other end. They go against the offensive player who took the shot or turned the ball over if there was no shot attempt. The two players on offense again make a quick attack at the single defender, passing the ball until there is a driving lane available. The player with the driving lane takes the ball hard to the basket until contact, before he thinks about dropping the ball off. The second offensive player should be getting inside rebounding position on the lone defender for an offensive rebound.

The two original offensive players, who did not shoot the first shot or turn the ball over, stay on the defensive end and become the two defenders waiting for the next three offensive players to attack. In Diagram 49b, the rebounder was the player who took the first shot, so he retreats to defend the 2-on-1, while the other two players stay at that end for defense.

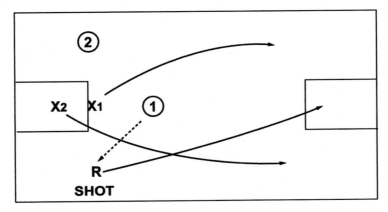

Diagram 49b.

Drill 50 — 3-on-2 – 2-on-2 – 2-on-1 - 1-on-1

Objectives:

- To practice having a numerical advantage on offense.
- To practice a 2-on-2 ball screen (offense and defense).
- To practice 1-on-1 full court (offense and defense).
- To provide conditioning.

Description:

There are four transitions in this drill for some players. The first transition (Diagram 50a) is the same as the previous drill with three offensive players going down the court against two established defenders.

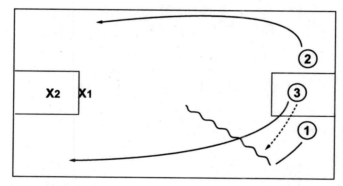

Diagram 50a.

In this drill, the player who takes the first shot or turns the ball over (O1) stays on the defensive end, while O2 and O3 retreat on defense (Diagram 50b). X1 and X2 convert to offense and go down the court for a two-on-two against O2 and O3 in this case. This is an opportunity for the offense and the defense to practice the techniques required offensively and defensively with screens on the ball.

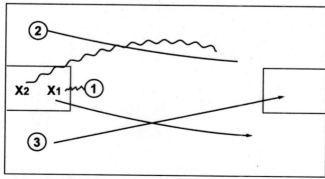

Diagram 50b.

In the third transition (Diagram 50c), the non-shooter X2 is retreating to play defense on O2 and O3, who are working on attacking the basket 2-on-1. The fourth transition (Diagram 50d) may be the most difficult, especially when the players are tired. In this transition, X2 is on defense attempting to stop O2 and O3. If O2 takes the first shot, O3 will be the next defender. His job is to pick up and control the dribbler (X2), forcing him to the sideline or to change directions as many times as possible before getting into the scoring area. Once in the half-court, O3 plays solid one-on-one defense while X2 attempts to score.

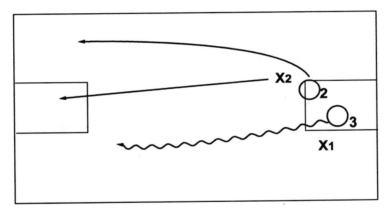

Diagram 50c.

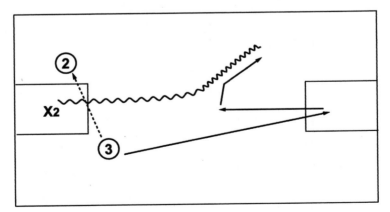

Diagram 50d.

Drill 51 — 4-on-4 Touch the Line

Objective:

- To practice quickly identifying the open players in a 4-on-3 situation.

Description:

The coach lines up four offensive players and four defensive players across the foul-line extended in the back court. The coach starts with the ball under the basket and can throw an unguarded pass to any of the four offensive players. On the pass, all four offensive players attack the offensive end. When the offensive player catches the first pass from the coach, the player defending that player must touch the baseline before getting back on defense. The other three defensive players dive back and attempt to delay the offense until their fourth defender can arrive, and they can get matched up.

The goal of the offense is to get a good shot attempt while they have a numerical advantage. If they are unable to accomplish that goal, they settle into their half-court offensive scheme. One of the objectives of this drill is to help players recognize when they have a fast break opportunity and when they do not.

The coach can use several methods to modify this drill including:

- Send two defenders to the baseline so that the offense is 4-on-2.

- Start one defender on the defensive end and run three defenders from the baseline; the offense gets a 15-foot head start.

- The coach can throw the ball to a non-decision maker and force him to make a second pass to a player who is a decision-maker on the way down the floor.

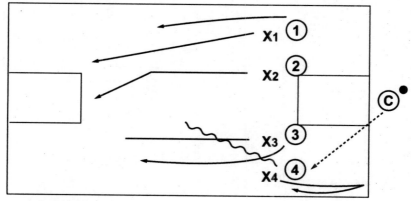

Diagram 51.

Drill 52 — Recognition Drill – When Do you Go and When Do You Whoa

Objective:

- To have players practice recognizing when they have a numerical advantage and when they do not.

Description:

Three offensive players start in back court, and the coach outlets the ball, which signals them to go on the break. The coach at half-court on the sideline stands with the defenders and sends out, one, two, three, or four defenders. The responsibility of the three offensive players, particularly the decision-maker, is to identify quickly if the offense has an advantage or not and react accordingly. If the defense sends out four players, they can trap the ball. The offensive team plays out the sequence until they score or lose the ball.

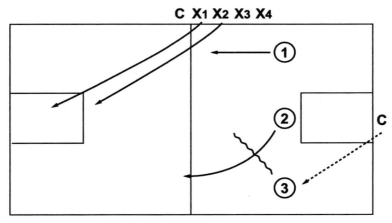

Diagram 52.

Drill 53 — Three Teams — 4-on-2 Exchange

Objectives:

- To practice a quick offensive attack when a two-player advantage exists.
- To practice getting a good first shot and then offensive rebounding.

Description:

The coach selects three teams of four players each, each with two ballhandlers and two wing or post players. In this drill, the coach needs to use three different colors of scrimmage vests to distinguish the teams. In Diagram 53a, the four members of the blue team go against green #3 and #4. As soon as green team rebounds, steals, or gets scored on, green #1 and #2 step in to the outlet spots, and green goes on the attack against the red defenders (#3 and #4). The blue team stays on the end of the floor where they were just on offense. They place the guards on the sideline ready to step in for an outlet, while the blue forwards play defense against the red team. The goal of the offensive team is to get a good first shot going toward the basket, and if the shot is not made, they should be able to out-rebound the two defenders with all four offensive players. The offense should score almost every time in this drill. A coach can be positioned under the basket on each end to evaluate each offensive attack. The importance of aggressively getting into position to get an offensive rebound and a second shot attempt should be reinforced.

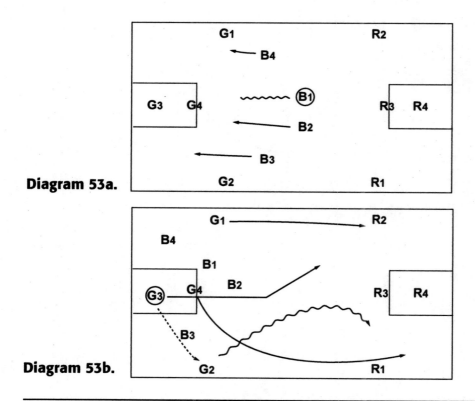

Diagram 53a.

Diagram 53b.

Drill 54 — 5-on-3 — Three-Team Exchange

Objective:

- To practice the basic cuts and reads for teams that run a pattern fast break.

Description:

This drill is similar to the 4-on-2 drill previously described. This time, each team has all five players on the offensive end going against three defenders. The three defenders can play a triangle zone or just scramble. For teams that run a pattern or numbered fast break, the players get shooting and decision-making opportunities from their designated, predetermined spots.

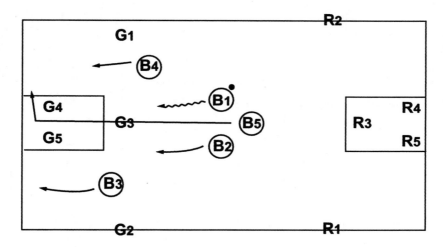

Diagram 54.

Drill 55 — Three-Man Hustle

Objectives:

- To practice passing, catching, and shooting at full speed.

- To improve the fitness level of the team.

Description:

This drill can be conducted early in practice as warm-up running, or at the end of practice to work on the fundamentals of passing, catching, and shooting when players are fatigued. This is a pattern drill, meaning that each line runs a specific route. Encourage each player to learn the pattern of one of the lines before they try to switch lines.

The ball should never hit the floor in this drill. If it is dropped or dribbled, that threesome stops where they are and goes to the end of the line. On the first trip down the floor (Diagram 55a), O1 starts with the ball in the middle and hits O3 on the move, and gets a return pass as he is *sprinting* up court. After catching the return pass, he kicks the ball ahead to O2, who has been streaking down the right lane. O2 must catch the ball and lay it in without having the ball hit the floor. After O3 has made the return pass to O1, he *sprints* to the basket to rebound O2's shot *before it hits the floor*. After O1 has made the long pass to O2 for the lay in, he *sprints* to the right side to touch the baseline with his hand.

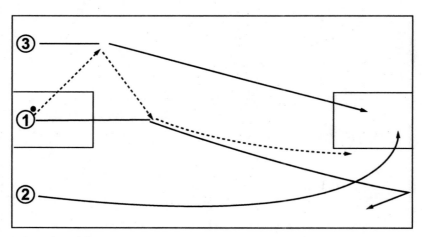

Diagram 55a.

The return trip begins immediately (Diagram 55b). After O2 has shot his lay in, he circles through to the sideline and gets the outlet pass from O3. After catching the outlet, he returns the ball back to O3 and sprints to the far basket to rebound the next shot. After O3 has rebounded the ball out of the basket, he outlets to O2 and then gets the return pass. He then hits O1 on the dead run for the lay in. O1, after touching the baseline, must turn and take off if he is going to get far enough down the floor to catch and shoot without dribbling. Be aware of your players traveling if they have to wait for another player to get down court. Traveling counts the same as the ball touching the floor.

To make this drill more difficult, the following challenges can be incorporated:

- See how many total team baskets are made in two minutes.

- Go until the team makes 10 or 20 in a row without a miss.

- If the focus is on conditioning, have your players make two trips up and down the floor. If you look at where the players end when they have completed their trip back (Diagram 55b), O1 is shooting the ball, and in the middle of the court, O2 is rebounding the shot. O2 can hand the ball back to O1 before he circles through and starts his sprint up the right side. O3 sprints back to the baseline where he first started the drill and turns back up court for the outlet pass.

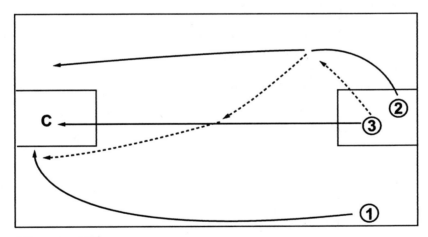

Diagram 55b.

Drill 56 — Continuous Decision Making — 3-on-2 to 3-on-1

Objectives:

- To give continuous repetitions to the point guards.

- To provide repetitions of fast break shooting for the wings.

- To improve individual and team conditioning.

Description:

This drill is an excellent warm-up for the beginning of practice or a great way to end practice, trying to execute fundamental skills when the players are tired. It tests the ability of your point guard and your other decision-maker type players. They must continually run, handle, and make decisions to get the ball to their shooters.

One point guard (O1) starts with a ball and two teammates. The threesome is going against two defenders (3-on-2 at the end of the court). The other point guards are waiting to trade in at half-court on the sideline (Diagram 56a). The rest of the players line up in each of the four corners of the court and as they get to the front of the line, go on the fast-break attack with the point guard. They attempt to finish and rebound before they go to the end of one of the lines in the corners.

A coach stands on each side of the court with a ball. As soon as O1 has made the first pass on the offensive attack, the coach on that sideline throws him the ball so he can immediately turn and go 3-on-1 to the other end (Diagram 56b). As soon as the ball comes in to O1, the next two wing players come out of the corner and go to the far end.

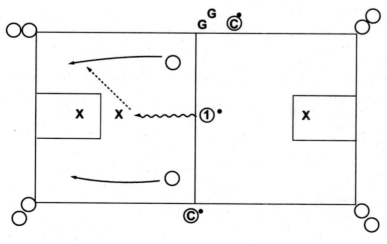

Diagram 56a.

This procedure continues for a specified amount of time or number of transitions, and then the coach calls for the next point guard to come in from the sideline. The challenge for the point guards is to keep up their speed, while continuing to make solid decisions with the ball.

Change defenders on both ends of the court when you change point guards.

The following methods can be employed to increase the difficulty of this drill:

- Continue until the entire team has scored 40 baskets, all on their first shots

- Have the same point guard stay on the floor until the team has scored 10 times

- Have the point guard stay on as long as he physically can and then have him take himself out when he is too fatigued to make good decisions

- Have the point guard only stay on until his team turns the ball over once or doesn't get a first shot. This type of emphasis will ensure that the focus is on making the simplest decision and getting the ball to players who can catch and shoot.

- See how many scores the combined team can get in four minutes at or near the beginning of practice, and then see if they can equal or better that total at the end of practice.

- Set the drill up so the offense goes against two defenders on each end

- Put a stopwatch on each transition and require that the point guard catch, advance and deliver the ball in four seconds. This stipulation will not only speed up the point guard, but also make the wings really have to sprint to get ahead of the ball each time.

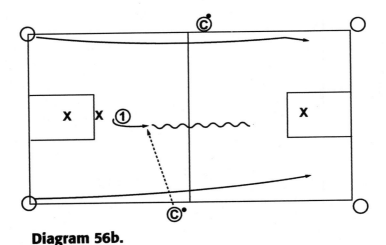

Diagram 56b.

Drill 57 — 5-on-5 Break and Counter Break

Objectives:

- To practice the secondary fast break, including making proper cuts and reads.

Description:

Two teams of five players each begin with a one-shot free-throw situation. If the blue team is shooting, they will hustle back on defense and match up with the red team. Whether they get scored on or not, they will counter break back to the end where they started. The red team starts on free-throw defense and runs their break whether the free throw is made or missed. Each team will look for the early break, but most often will have to run their "secondary" fast break pattern. After one transition in each direction, the coach should stop and evaluate each fast break.

If the secondary break is being emphasized, the coach can insist that each team get a shot off the secondary pattern. If the offensive team cannot get a shot after the pattern has been completed, the coach will blow the whistle, and the offensive team will place the ball down on the floor and hustle back to defense. This will force each team to work hard on the secondary pattern if they want to score. If you are working on a quick attack, you can operate this drill with a 7-to-10 second shot clock.

To add difficulty to the drill, a coach can have each team make two transitions after starting with a free throw. It is important that you do not have so many transitions that you lose the focus of the drill.

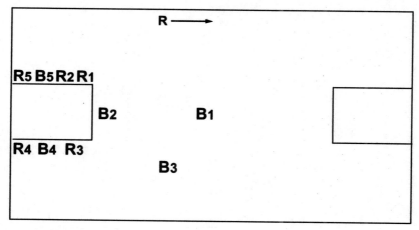

Diagram 57.

CHAPTER 6

TEAM OFFENSIVE DRILLS

Overview

An unlimited number of offensive basketball drills exist that coaches can select to work on during practice. Each coach should choose an offense that best utilizes the skills of his team members. The coach needs to understand all of the fundamentals involved for each player, at each position. I would encourage you to look at the offense you have chosen for your team and then break it down into teachable parts. Each part or option becomes its own drill. All of your offensive drills should apply directly to the principles and fundamentals required to correctly execute your specific offense. It is essential that you can analyze your own offensive scheme and understand how to break it down so that your players comprehend it as well as they should.

When teaching a skill, pattern, or offense for the first time, the coach should identify it by a name, a number, or some recognizable key. Then, use this term every time you refer to the skill. Begin by slowly demonstrating the whole pattern and calling each part by name. Then, identify and drill each part of the pattern required to properly execute the bigger picture. Gradually increase the speed of the demonstration and drills, and begin to put the pieces together at game speed. Give your players a written handout to read or at least visually remind them of the separate parts, the terms, and the whole picture, so that when they return the following day, they will be prepared to move ahead.

At the practice sessions that follow, quickly repeat the procedure and then begin *teaching, correcting, reinforcing and shaping* the physical skills of your players. Players need to understand the exact objectives of every drill. When first teaching offenses, it is important to provide opportunities in practice for the players to be successful.

Drill 58 – How to Devise Your Own Offensive Drills

Objectives:

- To demonstrate how to design an offensive drill.

Description:

The primary goal of this drill is to teach coaches how to diagram a specific play (Diagram 58a) and then to show coaches how to break the play down and devise their own drills to duplicate the individual parts of the play (Diagrams 58a to 58c). Once an offense is broken down into teachable parts, a coach should to look at the exact fundamentals involved in the offense and understand how he can demonstrate, explain, drill and correct those fundamentals.

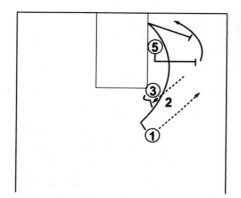 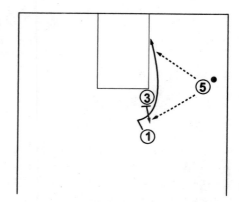

Diagram 58a.   **Diagram 58b.**

Even though it only involves three players, the play in Diagram 58a may appear very complex to your players when they look at the whole diagram. But when the play is broken down into the following teachable parts, it become much simpler:

- A wing entry pass, timed with the approach of the point guard.

- A "post rub" by O1 off O3's screen.

- A step back off the high post screen and pass to O3.

- O1 steps out to back screen for O5.

Each of these parts has options, reads, and smaller-detail fundamentals that can be taught, corrected, and executed by breaking them down into teachable drills.

Diagram 58a – Wing-entry pass

This section of the offense involves the following fundamentals:

(1) Timing of the cutters (O3 and O5) to coincide with the approach of the dribbler (O1) so that the spacing of the first pass is correct.

(2) O5 being able to "L" out to get open without the use of a screen.

(3) O5 catching the ball and getting squared up against a pressure defender, and carrying the threat of a drive.

Other options in this part of the offense that can be offered when your players are ready include:

- Out of the stack, O3 circles to the outside of O5 and cuts first to provide a better opportunity to get himself open.

- O1 passing to O3, and O5 cutting backdoor.

- O1 ball faking to O5 and passing to him as he cuts backdoor.

Diagram 58b – Post rub

This section of the offensive pattern includes the following fundamentals:

(1) O1 "V" cuts away to set up his defender and then makes a quick change-of-direction cut off O3's hip.

(2) O1 looks for the return pass as he clears the screener.

(3) O3 pivots and sets a screen with his back by pivoting out toward O1 and staying stationary.

(4) By screening with his back, O3 faces the basket and can see how far off his defender is going hedge to help on O1's cut.

(5) O3 then pops back to the three-point line, ready to receive the pass from O5 if O1 is not open on the rub cut.

(6) O5 reads the screen at the high post to see if O1's defender has been picked off and then to see if O3's defender hedges to help. He must make the decision, if the cutter is open early, to get O1 the ball on his way to the basket or reverse the ball back to O3.

Other options available in this portion of the offensive pattern include:

- O1 can cut on the backside of O3.

- O1 can fake the cut and step back if his defender cheats and drops back below the screen too quickly.

- O1 can post up at the block if he has an advantage.

- If O3 is a three-point shooter, he should think "shot" as he catches the reversal pass from O5.

Diagram 58c – Back pick the perimeter

This portion of the offensive pattern includes the following fundamentals:

(1) After O5 has reversed the ball to O3, he sets his defender up and comes off a back screen set by O1, goes to the block, and posts.

(2) O1 steps out of the block and sets a hard back screen for O5 (a small player screening big player). He then pops off the screen to the three-point line for a return pass and possible shot.

(3) O3 has the ball and reads the back screen. He can pass either to O5 who is cutting to the basket, or to O1 who is stepping off the screen to the three-point line.

Additional options that can be taught in this part of the pattern include:

- O5 can come off the screen and post up on the block for a high-low pass from O3 or a wing-entry pass from O1.

- If O3 hits O1 on the wing, the whole pattern can begin again with O5 going to the high post to screen for O3 making a post rub cut to the basket.

The aforementioned is just one example of taking a short offensive pattern or play and breaking it down into teachable parts, and then devising drills that teach exactly how the skill should appear in a game. Once broken down, the coach must identify the fundamentals and understand how to correct them. He should gradually put the pieces together until his players can perform the screens, cuts, and reads at game speed. This same method can be used for any complex skill or pattern.

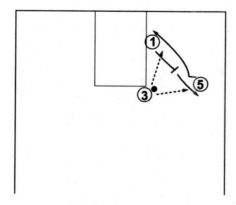

Diagram 58c.

OVERVIEW

Drills 59 – 61 – Setting Screens

Objective:

• To practice the fundamentals of setting screens.

Description:

Coaches or players with blocking shields are defending the players receiving the screen, and are the target for the screener. The rotation is from screener to receiver; the new player comes in as the next screener.

Coaching Points:

• "Squaring up on the target" so the middle of the screeners chest is on the near shoulder of the target player.

• The screener needs to provide enough space to be legal; the screener should not initiate the contact.

• The screener must establish a strong stance without exaggerating his feet, knees, or upper body to create contact with the target player.

• The screener can call "go" when he is ready for the cutter to use the screen.

• The screener needs to learn to set the screen at an angle that allows the cutter to get open where you want him to go. The cutter should get open going in the direction of the screener's back.

Drill 59 – Down Screens

Objective:

- To practice the fundamentals involved in setting a down screen.

Description:

The players setting the screen follow the fundamentals previously described.

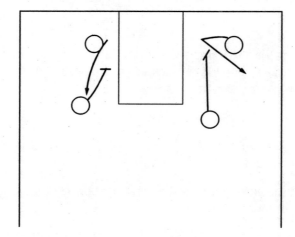

Diagram 59.

Drill 60 — Setting Back Screens

Objective:

- To practice the fundamentals of setting a back screen.

Description:

The positioning of the players and the targets for drilling back screens are shown in Diagram 60. Both the screener and receiver use the fundamentals previously described.

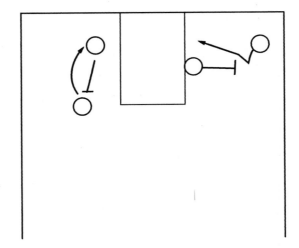

Diagram 60.

Drill 61 — Setting Cross Screens

Objective:

- To practice the fundamentals of setting cross screens.

Description:

The set up for a drill to practice cross screens is shown in Diagram 61. Players adhere to the fundamentals previously described for other types of screens.

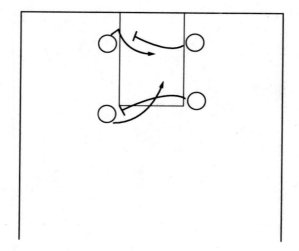

Diagram 61.

Drill 62 — Reading Screens

Objectives:

- To practice the fundamentals necessary for the cutter to come off the screen.

- To practice how to read the screen, and to move according to the direction the defender moves while playing the screen.

Description:

The set up is similar to the down-screen drill, with two coaches with blocking shields guarding the players on the block. As the screener comes down to set the screen, the offensive player "V" cuts in the opposite direction and sets his defender up. He tries to occupy his defender's vision with this preliminary movement. If the defender comes around the same side of the screen as the offensive player, the offensive player should "curl" the cut (Diagram 62a). If the defender goes on the opposite side of the screen as the offensive player, the offensive player should "flare" the screen (Diagram 62b). Cutting in this manner takes the defender further out of position.

Coaching Points:

- When first teaching this drill, allow the cutter to know ahead of time which way the defender is going to play the screen.

- As the cutter improves his ability to read, play the screen to either direction.

- Have the players waiting in line call out "curl" or " flare", depending on how they read the screen. This procedure will give each player even more mental repetitions.

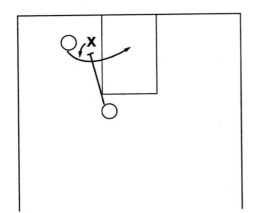

Diagram 62a.

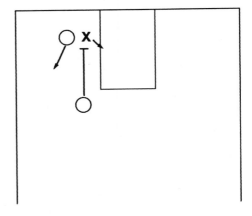

Diagram 62b.

Drill 63 — 2-On-2 Screening

Objective:

- To provide players with practice using the screening and reading techniques in a live situation while being defended.

Description:

The coach starts with a ball on the top of the three-point line. The two offensive players can either down screen or back screen to attempt to get open for a shot. If the ball is entered to the wing, the player at the block can post up. If a good shot is not available, they can always pass back to the coach and rescreen. The offensive players attempt to read each screen and make the appropriate cut. As they come off the screen they should try to signal for the ball with their voice, hands, and/or eyes.

Coaching Points:

- This exercise can become a competitive drill by allowing the defenders to go to offense if they do not give up a basket and do not foul.

- Advanced players should be able to verbalize "curl" or "flare" as they come off the screen, based upon how they see the defender play the screen.

- This drill can be used to focus on any specific type of screen.

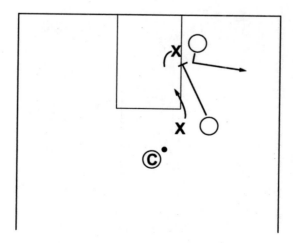

Diagram 63.

Drill 64 — 3-on-3 Screening — One Side of the Floor

Objective:

- To practice live screening and reading techniques, while adding a post for a cross screen or flash.

Description:

This drill is set up the same as the 2-on-2 drill, except for the fact that a third player is added on the opposite post. As the ball is entered to the wing, the player who has screened down to start the offensive movement can now screen across the key (Diagram 64a). This procedure teaches the concept of continuing to screen. The players can fill any of the three spots and can post up, as well as come off screens to get a shot. The only limitation is that they cannot go to the far side of the court to catch the ball.

The player on the opposite post can flash to the high post (Diagram 64b) under any of the following situations:

- Any time the coach is having trouble entering the ball to the wing.

- If the player on the low block is being fronted or denied the ball from the wing, he can flash to the high post to make the high-low entry pass.

Note: When the ball is caught at the high post, the player at the low block can also set a back screen for the wing player.

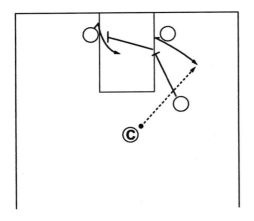

Diagram 64a.

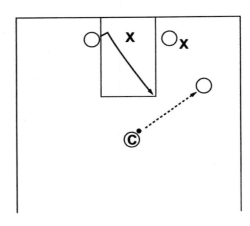

Diagram 64b.

Drill 65 — 4-on-4 – Score Two out of Three

Objective:

- To practice the setting and reading of screens and attempting to score to stay on offense.

Description:

The four players on offense can place themselves at any of the two perimeter positions or two inside positions. The coach stays in one spot, and the four offensive players must include him in their spacing (Diagram 65a). The ball can be passed to the coach at any time, and he can pass to any of the offensive players on the floor. The four offensive players can use any of the various types of screens. The four defenders attempt to keep the offense from scoring. The goal of the offensive team is to score on two out of three possessions. If they do, they stay on offense against the next four players, and the defensive team waits out. If they do not succeed in scoring two out of three possessions, the defensive team gets to go on offense, and the next team comes in on defense.

Coaching Points:

- The coach can choose to stand in different areas of the floor (Diagram 65b) to change the spacing used by the four offensive players.

- Fouls count as a score.

- To encourage screening, the coach should not throw the ball to any player unless he is coming off a screen.

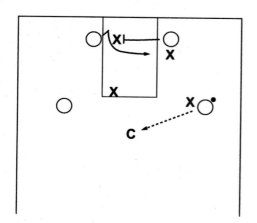

Diagram 65a.

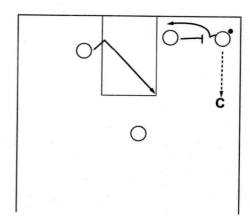

Diagram 65b.

Drill 66 — 4-on-4 – Quick Change

Objectives:

- To practice setting and using screens in the half-court.

- To practice making a quick transition from offense to defense.

Description:

The set up for this drill is the same as the previous drill, with four offensive players going against four defenders and a team of four waiting on the baseline to come in on defense. The coach can station himself in a position to always be a safety valve. In order to make it more competitive and require quicker transitions, if the offensive team does not score, they immediately convert to defense. The team that was on defense and got the defensive rebound, steal, or turnover *immediately* passes the ball to the coach and then goes to offense. As soon as either team scores, that team stays on offense, and the defense leaves the floor and is replaced by the team waiting on the baseline.

The quickness of the transition from defense-to-offense can produce easy scores if the new defensive team is hanging their head or worried about the mistake they just made on offense. The coach should not pass the ball to anyone unless he is coming off a screen. Players will learn to begin the offensive movement with a screen instead of standing begging for the ball.

It should be noted this drill can become very competitive and does not provide any time for players who need time to recover from their mistakes. If you are trying to use this as an aggressiveness drill, allow your players to set hard screens and to rebound without calling too many fouls.

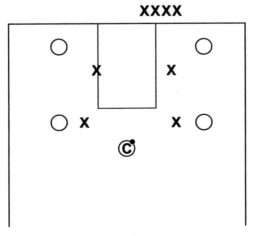

Diagram 66.

Drill 67 — 5-on-5 Offense

Objective:

- To practice your half-court offense with all five players.

Description:

After you have broken down the offense into its teachable parts and are ready to reconstruct it into 5-on-5 basketball, always use some form of emphasis to keep the team focused and to get them to perform at game speed. If you are attempting to rehearse the pattern, let them go 5-on-0, but if the goal is to execute the offense, give them some goals that are measurable.

Among the possible points of emphasis or limitations that can be used when practicing half-court 5-on-5 are the following:

- In order to stay on offense, that team must score two out of three or three out of five possessions.

- In order to stay on offense, the shot must be from a specific spot on the court.

- The shot must be taken by a specific player or position.

- The first shot has to be off of a specific type of screen.

- No shots can be attempted until all players have touched the ball.

- No shots can be attempted until the post has touched the ball.

- No shots can be attempted until the ball has been reversed.

- Do not allow any shots, but rather have the player call "shot" when he has one that he thinks is a good team shot off the offense and just continue playing offense.

- There must be a shot fake or a pass fake used before a team shoots for the first time.

- No dribbling.

- The person shooting the ball must verbalize his cut or his shot doesn't count.

Which emphasis you choose depends on which offensive fundamental you want your team to focus on. Identify what areas of offense need the most work and make that area your emphasis for that particular section of the offensive practice.

CHAPTER 7

SHOOTING DRILLS

Overview

When choosing which shooting drills to use in practice, the coach should design drills that simulate the shots that their players are likely to get in a game situation. Once good shooting form has been acquired by individual players, a shooting drill is only beneficial if it is performed at the same speed and distances that will be used in a game.

The drills illustrated in this chapter are ones that have been effectively used for all age groups. Only the distances and positions on the floor need to be altered to accommodate different age groups and ability levels.

Drill 68 — Shoot and Follow

Objectives:

- To provide players practice shooting and then following their own shots.

- To provide players practice following the shots of their teammates.

- To teach players to practice anticipating the rebounding angles.

Description:

Players are divided into two lines. In one line, each player has a ball and shoots as he moves to the front of the line. The shooter follows his shot toward the basket. The other line (Diagram 68a) lines up about 15 feet from the basket. As soon as the shooter releases the ball, the first player in the rebounding line runs to rebound, along with the shooter. The goal is for either of the players to get the ball before it hits the floor. When the ball is caught, each of the players must make a lay in (i.e., follow-up the shot). They are trying to make three shots in rapid succession. A perfect repetition of this drill would be for the first player to make his shot, have the rebounder get the ball before it hits the floor, and then have both players make a lay-in before the ball touches the floor. In Diagram 68b, the shooting line is on the wing, making the rebound angle change. Coaches should choose shooting spots that coincide with their offense.

If the coach wants to make it more competitive, have the two players battle for the ball. The one that doesn't get the rebound plays defense. They continue to play until one player scores.

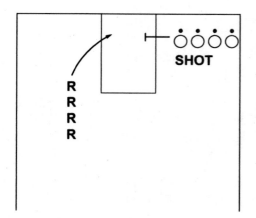

Diagram 68a.

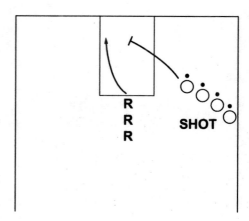

Diagram 68n.

Drill 69 — Partner and Ball – Shoot and Follow

Objectives:

- To practice following a player's own shot.

- To practice making an accurate pass to the shooter.

- To improve conditioning and shooting on the move.

Description:

The drill involves two players who are teamed up and a ball. The first player shoots and follows his shot, gets the rebound, and passes back to his partner who is moving to the ball. They continue attempting to make as many shots as possible in the time allotted. This shooting drill can last thirty seconds to one minute.

Coaching Points:

- Shooters should receive the ball in a flexed, "ready shoot" position.

- Shooters should move into the shooting areas where they get their shots in the half-court offense.

- Players should move quickly from shooter, to rebounder, to passer, to shooter.

- To add difficulty to the drill, the coach can have the shooter follow up and make any missed shot.

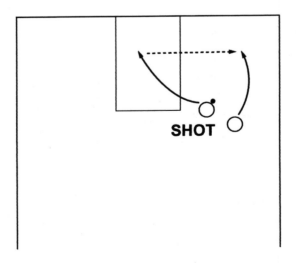

Diagram 69.

Drill 70 — Ball and a Partner Close Out

Objectives:

- To provide shooting repetitions.

- To practice shooting over a "hand up".

- To practice following a player's own shot.

- To practice defensive close outs.

Description:

Player O1 shoots the ball and follows his shot. He rebounds the ball and passes it back out to O2. On the pass, O1 closes out on O2 and contests the shot. O2 then follows his shot and closes out on O1 as he passes the ball out. Each shooter moves to a new location after each close out. If you are more concerned about shooting while being contested than you are in working on your defensive close outs, then the player running out on the shooter can try to break the shooter's concentration by jumping and "flying by".

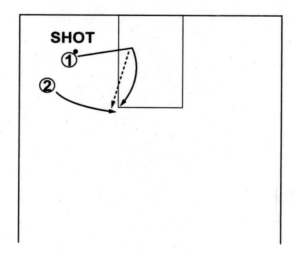

Diagram 70.

Drill 71 — Kick Out "Double"

Objectives:

- To practice feeding the post position.

- To practice moving after the ball is entered to the post.

- To practice verbalizing and calling for the ball.

- To practice a quick release of the shot.

Description:

A coach gets in the low-post area and targets the ball with his hands. The first player in line passes the ball to the coach on the block, trying to put the ball directly in the coach's "target hand". As soon as the ball is entered, the perimeter player imagines that his defender has doubled down on the post. If his man covers down, the offensive perimeter player's responsibility is to move to a new location and call "double". He moves so that the defender cannot come automatically back out to the same spot and find him. He calls "double" so that the post is alerted that he is being double-teamed and where the open man is located.

The post (coach) kicks that ball back out to the perimeter man, who shoots, follows his shot, and goes to the opposite line. The shooter should attempt to catch the ball in a "ready shoot" position so that he can get the shot off quickly. Each shooting drill should challenge the shooters to see how many quality shots they can get away in the time allotted.

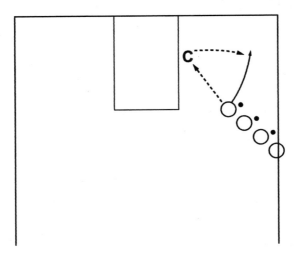

Diagram 71.

Drill 72 — Kick Out "Flare" – Zone Shots

Objectives:

- To practice feeding the ball to the high post.

- To practice moving to the open area at the bottom of the zone.

- To practice verbalizing "flare".

- To practice a quick release of an attempted shot.

- To practice following an attempted shot.

Description:

A feeder starts with a ball on the point and passes to a coach at the high post. As the coach catches the ball, the player on the wing flares toward the corner. He calls "flare" and spots up for a kick-out pass from the high-post player. He catches the ball in a flexed, "ready shoot" position and quickly gets his shot away.

This is a shot that offenses can often get from any zone offense. As the high post catches the ball, he should turn and face the basket. This opens up his vision to the bottom of the court. The shooter on the wing needs to slide down within his vision and call for the ball. As the perimeter player moves down toward the baseline, he needs to be aware of the baseline zone defenders and where they have rotated to cover. Players go from the passing line to the shooting spot on the wing.

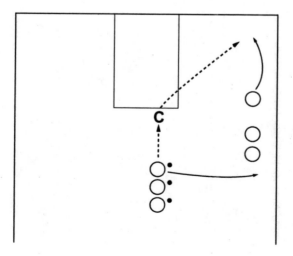

Diagram 72.

Drill 73 — Three Players, Two Basketballs

Objectives:

- To practice game-speed shots.
- To practice accuracy in passing.
- To practice anticipating the rebound.

Description:

Players get into groups of three with two basketballs. Player O1 is the first shooter. O2 is the passer, and O3 is the rebounder. O3 attempts to get each rebound as quickly as he can and get the ball to O2 immediately after he has passed the other ball. O2 tries to get a ball into the hands of the shooter as quickly as he can after the shooter has moved and is showing his hands. O1 shoots, "v cuts", and shows his hands when he is ready for the next ball (Diagram 73a). He is working on shooting at game speed from the places on the floor where he will most likely get his shots from the offense during a game situation.

After 30 seconds, the coach whistles, and the players rotate from shooter to rebounder, rebounder to passer, and passer to the next shooter. Diagram 73b shows the rotation. O1 is the new rebounder, O3 is the new passer and O2 is the new shooter. When the players hear the whistle, the shooter fakes the outside shot and drives to the basket, signaling the rotation. The coach can also have the players change on their own, after making a specified number of shots.

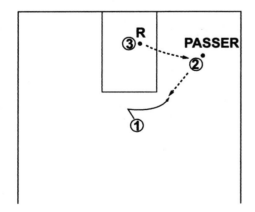

Diagram 73a.

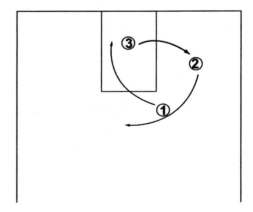

Diagram 73b.

CHAPTER 8

PASSING AND
PRE-GAME DRILLS

Drill 74 — Five Star Passing

Objectives:

- To practice passing and receiving the ball.

- To learn a pre-game, warm-up drill.

Description:

Players divide into five even lines around the circle. One ball is used for this drill. It can be in the front of any of the five lines. If there is not an even number of players, the line that begins with the ball should have the extra player. The player with the ball passes to the first player two lines to his left and then hustles to the end of that line, going to the left of that line. The receivers continue to pass two lines to their left, moving quickly to that line. If they follow by running to the right, there is a chance that they will be hit with the ball as it is being passed in a star formation.

Coaches can vary the distance of the circle or the type of pass the players are required to throw. Examples of modifications that can be made to this drill include:

- Bounce passes only.

- Overhead passes only.

- Precede the pass with a ball fake in the opposite direction.

- Move in closer, jump, catch, and shoot the ball before the player hits the floor.

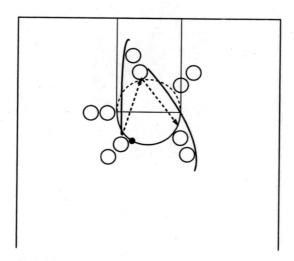

Diagram 74.

Drill 75 — Two Post Passing

Objectives:

- To practice passing and receiving the ball.

- To learn a pre-game, warm-up drill.

Description:

Two post players are positioned at the elbows, each with a basketball. Two lines of the remaining players are evenly divided, facing each other about 15-to-20 feet apart with one ball that will be passed back and forth between the two lines. O1 starts with a ball and passes to O2; O1 then follows his pass toward the far post (O9). O9 passes his ball to O1, who then quickly returns the pass to O9 and goes to the end of the opposite line. O2, who initially received the ball from O1, then passes to O3 and follows toward O10 to receive and return a pass from O10. After returning the ball to O10, O2 goes to the end of the opposite line.

The three basketballs used in this drill should almost constantly be in the air as the players move quickly from one pass to the next. The type of passes and the distances involved in the passes can be varied.

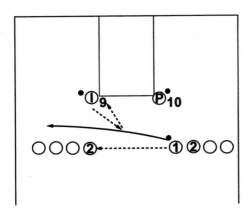

Diagram 75a.

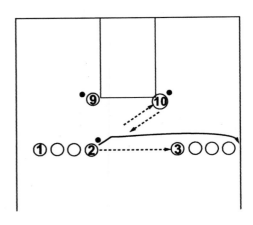

Diagram 75b.

Drill 76 — Peripheral Vision Passing

Objectives:

- To practice passing and receiving the ball.

- To improve peripheral vision.

Description:

In Diagram 76a, three players form a triangle, and have two basketballs. Two of the players (O1 and O2) are required to maintain eye contact with each other, while the third player (O3) keeps both of the other two insight. The two basketballs are passed clockwise by the three players. By having O1 and O2 maintain eye contact, they are forced to use their peripheral vision while passing and catching. The players should rotate positions every 15-30 seconds.

Diagram 76b illustrates expanding this drill to use five players and two basketballs. The players form two triangles, and the basketballs are passed in a clockwise rotation. All passes go through O3, with O1 and O2, and O4 and O5 maintaining constant eye contact with each other while the basketballs are being passed. Coaches should have the players rotate positions every 15 to 30 seconds. The coach can also require the players to change the direction of the passes.

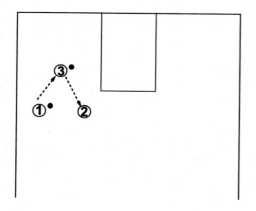

Diagram 76a.

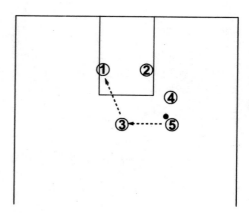

Diagram 76b.

Drill 77 — Four-Corner Passing

Objective:

- To practice passing and shooting.

- To engage in a pre-game, warm-up drill.

Description:

The drill begins with four, evenly balanced lines in the corners of the half-court. The basketball starts with O1. The ball goes from O1 to O2, and from O2 to O3, with a two-hand chest pass. O3 passes to O4 using a bounce pass, and O4 passes to O1, who is cutting for a lay in, using a bounce pass or a flip pass. After O1 makes his first pass, he cuts around the outside of O2 and times his cut to receive the ball, cutting at full speed from O4 for the lay-in. After O2 has made his pass, he follows to the foul line to wait for a pass from the rebounder (O4). After receiving the outlet pass from the rebounder, O2 pivots and passes back out to the line where the drill began, and the next four players continue the drill. The players rotate lines from O1 to O2, from O2 to O3, from O3 to O4, and from O4 to O1.

To add difficulty to the drill, the following steps can be undertaken:

- Switch directions and have your players shoot from the left side of the basket.

- See how many shots your players can make in a specified time – placing an emphasis on quick, accurate passes and catches.

- Add a second basketball – the next ball can start as soon as the previous ball is being shot.

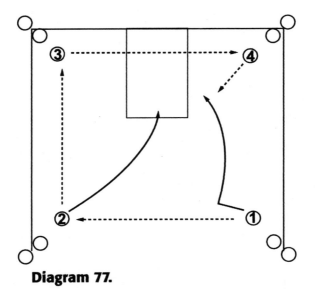

Diagram 77.

Drill 78 — Five Out, 3-on-2 In

Objectives:

- To engage in a pre-game, warm-up drill.

- To practice passing and shooting in a 3-on-2 situation.

Description:

Players line up in five lines on the baseline of their basket. The middle line has a basketball. As the player in the middle begins to dribble the ball to mid-court, the other four players all sprint to mid-court (Diagram 78a). As soon as they reach the mid-court line, all five players turn and go toward the basket. Players in lines 1, 3 and 5 are on offense, while players in lines 2 and 4 are on defense (Diagram 78b). The players complete the 3-on- 2 situation, using the fundamentals learned in Chapter 5.

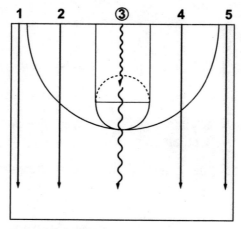

Diagram 78a.

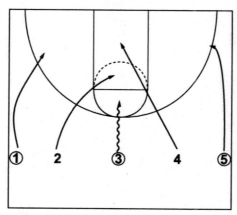

Diagram 78b.

Drill 79 – Three-Man Weave – All Three Shoot

Objective:

- To engage in a pre-game, warm-up drill that involves passing, receiving and shooting.

Description:

Two players (O4 and O5) are on the baseline, each with a basketball. The remaining players are in three lines near half-court. The middle line starts with a basketball (O1). They begin with a three-man weave toward the basket, passing and cutting behind the person to whom they passed the ball.

As O1 receives the ball back, he lays the ball in the basket, while the other two players continue in the direction they were running and receive a pass from the player in front of them on the baseline. They catch and shoot from the perimeter. After shooting, all three players rebound their own shot. The player shooting the lay-in returns the ball to the middle line, while the two players shooting a perimeter shot, keep the ball and go to the passing spots on the baseline. The next three players begin their weave toward the basket.

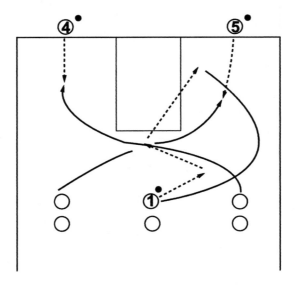

Diagram 79.

Drill 80 — Four Player - Speed Passing

Objective:

- To engage in a pre-game, warm-up drill.

Description:

Don't give up on this drill because it looks complicated. It is a great pre-game drill. Encourage your players to learn the drill from one of the four lines, before attempting to learn a second position (O2, and O3 are the easiest to learn). In each illustration (Diagrams 80a to 80c), O1 will start with the ball.

The players start in four even lines. Diagram 80a begins with O1 passing to O2 and then immediately cutting down the lane to screen for O4. As O4 is cutting across the key, O2 quickly passes to O3, who then passes across the key to O1. After passing, O2 moves to the high post, and O3 moves out to the top.

Diagram 80b begins with O1 passing across the key to O4, and then cutting back to his original position at the top. O4 passes to O2. O2 passes out to O3, who swings the ball to O1 at the top.

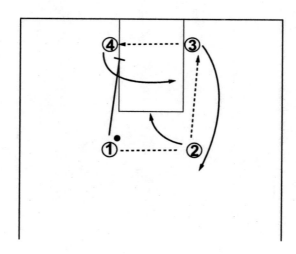

Diagram 80a.

In Diagram 80c, O1 passes to O2 and gets a quick return pass as he cuts to the basket. O1 lays the ball off the backboard, so the players that follow can continue tipping it to the player behind them. After O1 cuts, O3 is the next player peeling off the high post and tipping the ball off the backboard to the third player, O4. O4 tips the ball off the board to O2, who follows and "JAMS" the ball (or lays it in, if you have "normal" kids).

The players tip in the following order, O1, O3, O4, O2. If the players can learn the progression and the correct spacing (i.e., don't let them get too close together), the ball should be moved very quickly and efficiently until it is tipped in.

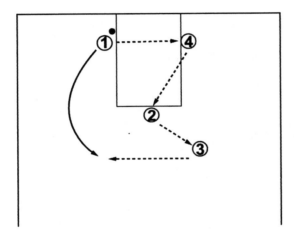

Diagram 80b.

TIP - TIP - TIP - LAY IN

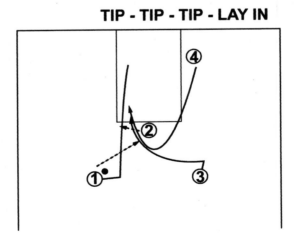

Diagram 80c.

Drill 81 – Five Player – Speed Passing and Tipping Drill

Objective:

- To engage in a pre-game, warm-up drill.

Description:

This drill is a little simpler than the previous one because it doesn't require quite as much player movement. In Diagram 81a, O4 starts with the ball on the wing and passes to O2. O2 quickly swings the ball to O1 and then follows his pass for a "hand back" and passes to O3. O2 continues to sprint to the outside of O3. As soon as O3 catches the ball, he passes to O5 at the high post.

Diagram 81b begins with O5 in possession of the ball at the high post. He passes out to O2, who has just circled outside of O3. O4 is the first cutter. He receives the ball and lays it off the backboard for the next player, O5. O3 screens up for O1 who "V" cuts and is the third person to tip the ball off the board. O3 follows off the screen and lays the ball in. O2 rebounds the ball and zips it out to the original line. Advanced teams can execute this drill to either side of the floor, depending on where the ball is passed out after the rebound.

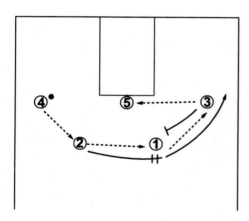

Diagram 81a.

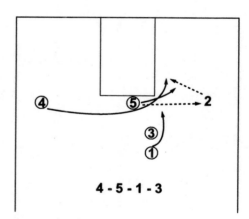

4 - 5 - 1 - 3

Diagram 81b.

CHAPTER 9

GAMES AND FUN WAYS
TO END PRACTICE
(LEAVE 'EM SMILING AND WANTING MORE)

You know it has been a productive and enjoyable practice when the players wish it was not over. They want to stay and play. They come up and ask for individual help. They want to shoot or practice their newly learned skills when they get home. In other words, they have fallen in love with the game. One of your primary goals as a coach should be to have as many players as possible learn to love the great game of basketball.

One of the most important skills a coach can develop is the ability to understand how to balance fun and discipline. Most discipline is often just "forced labor", and all fun often turns into silliness and is simply a waste of teaching and learning time. Many coaches think of themselves as being disciplinarians, by dealing out large amounts of yelling and punishment. An equal number of coaches, on the other extreme, confuse fun and silliness with achievement. The reality is that neither extreme is true. In athletics, having fun is getting better. Fun and discipline must be integrated or they both lose their value and effectiveness. Practically speaking, discipline is the ability to get and hold your players' attention, and receiving their best effort with regard to focusing on learning the skills that will help them improve as individual players and as a team.

One of the most important parts of communicating a "love of the game" to young players is the way the coach chooses to end practice. An effective coach finds methods to leave his team smiling and wanting more, instead of not being able to wait for practice to end. With a little planning, coaches can identify methods to conclude practice that are suitable for their specific age-group and will have players looking forward to the next practice session.

The simplest way to add some enthusiasm into any drill is to make it competitive. By simply keeping score in a drill, your players' energy and intensity levels will increase. If you chose to have different parts of the team compete against each other, find a way to reward the winners rather than punishing the team that lost. If you are trying to build team morale through competition, compete with the whole team against the clock or some pre-established standard. Most of all, the coach needs to allow himself to enjoy practice when it has been productive. Your players will take their cues from you with regard to what is fun and what is important. Always try to end practice on a positive note.

Drill 82 – Winner's Circle

Objective:

- To provide a chance to get players pulling for each other to achieve a goal against the clock.

Description:

Divide your team evenly at different baskets and set a realistic goal for your age group. After they have reached their objective at their basket, have them hustle and come join the coaches in the center circle of the court. The goal is to see if you can get the whole team into the winner's circle before time expires. For example, you may set a goal of having every player at each basket make two free throws in a row. As soon as all four people at that basket have made their two in a row, all four players head to the winner's circle, join the coach, and begin rooting for the teams that haven't completed the goal. The goal may be to see how long it takes to have everyone in the winner's circle, or to beat the time that had been established in a previous practice. Another goal would be to see how many players can be in the winner's circle in two minutes.

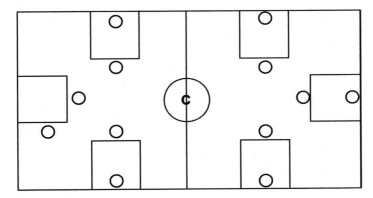

Diagram 82.

Other possible variations of this drill include:

- Having the team at each basket make a specified number of free throws, with each player shooting until he misses, if you do not want to put pressure on individual players.

- Requiring each player or team to make a three-pointer, a free throw, and a lay-in.

- Require each player to complete a combination of shots or skills and see which team gets to the winner's circle first.

Drill 83 — Three-Man Keep Away

Objective:

- To provide a competitive passing and defending drill.

Description:

Players divide into groups of three with one basketball per group. Two players get 15 feet apart, and the third gets in the middle. Once the coach signals for the predetermined allotted time period to start (e.g., 30-to-45 seconds), the two players attempt to pass the ball back and forth without letting the player in the middle get a deflection or a steal. The two passers cannot throw the ball above head height and must throw a pass that is caught without the receiver having to move his feet. The outside players must wait until the player in the middle has closed out on them before they pass, and they must get their pass off within five seconds of the close out. The outside players can pivot, but cannot dribble.

The player in the middle follows from passer to passer, attempting to touch one of the passes. After he has closed out, he counts out loud, five seconds, "5,4,3,2,1". When he begins counting, it is the signal that the offensive player can pass. This factor works on his defensive skills of challenging the passer on a "dead" dribble situation. As soon as a deflection, a steal, a five-second violation, or a bad pass occurs, the player who committed the infraction goes to the defensive (middle) position. The winners are the two people who are in the passing spots when time expires.

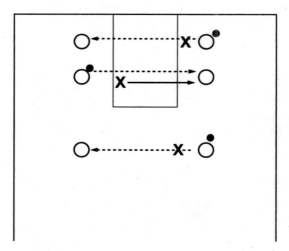

Diagram 83.

Drill 84 — Dribble Tag – Whole Court

Objective:

- To teach players to dribble with their heads and eyes up.

Description: Players get a partner and one basketball for the two of them. The coach can divide the players according to their abilities if necessary. One player goes out on the court with the ball, while his partner waits on the sideline. The coach names one of the players on the court "it". That player attempts to tag any of the other players while he has control of his dribble. The players not "it" must stay within specified boundaries. The first tagged player becomes "it", and attempts to catch another one of the players who is dribbling before time runs out (e.g., 30-to-45 seconds). At the end of time, the player who is "it" and his partner on the sideline are required to perform a specified number of pushups, and then the other half of the team comes on the floor to play. Players must keep their heads up to know who is "it" and to not collide with other moving players.

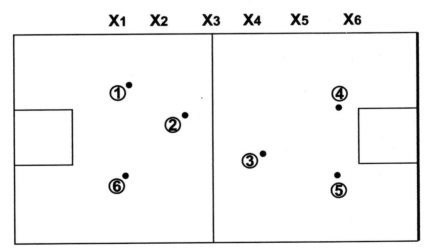

Diagram 84.

Possible variations of this drill include:

- The player who is "it" can dribble with either hand; the other players have to use their weak hand.

- The whole team can be involved in the drill simultaneously. Have two players be "it" and see how long it takes them to work together to catch all the other players. Once tagged, a player is out.

Drill 85 — Mixmaster

Objective:

- To teach players how to protect the ball while dribbling in traffic.

Description:

Divide your team so that one-third of them have a basketball and the others spread out in a designated area. The playing area should be large enough so that approximately 6-to-8 feet of space is between the non-dribblers when they are evenly spread out. The players without a basketball are limited as to how far they can move by having a pivot foot that cannot be dragged or changed. On the coach's signal, the players with the basketballs dribble into the maze and attempt to control their dribble, while using their opposite arm and body to protect the ball from the "defenders".

If the dribbler loses control of the ball and one of the defenders gets it, those players switch positions. You want your defenders to be aggressive with their hands, but not to the point of fouling. Challenge your dribblers to "stay in the mix" by going through the traffic at a quick pace and not resting in the open areas of the floor.

Players will have to keep their heads and eyes up to avoid collisions. They must dribble with both hands to keep the ball from being stolen, and constantly change direction while zigzagging through the "defenders". Because this is a tiring drill if performed correctly, three or four minutes should be a sufficient amount of time dedicated to this drill.

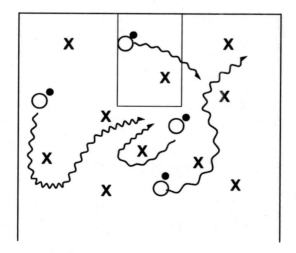

Diagram 85.

Drill 86 — Freeze Out

Objective:

- To practice competitive, pressure, free-throw shooting.

Description:

Players line up around the key and rotate through the line shooting one free throw at a time. The goal is to eliminate players one at a time until there is only one person left. A player is eliminated when he misses his free throw, and the player behind him makes his. If one player (O1) misses and the player behind him (O2) also misses, O1 is safe but O2 is eliminated if the next person makes his shot.

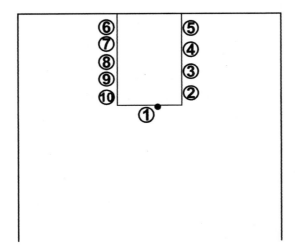

Diagram 86.

Possible variations of this drill include:

- Allowing the shooter to eliminate up to two players who have missed in front of him.

- Allowing the non-shooters to talk, sneeze, tease, cough, etc. to try to distract the shooter. They should not be allowed to make any contact or come inside the key or circle to distract the shooter.

- Having players who are shooting to eliminate someone be required to shoot with their eyes closed.

- Playing two separate games and have the two finalists represent their basket in a shootout. The team from each basket supports their representative.

Drill 87 — Thirty-One

Objectives:

- To practice competitive, rebounding, offensive attacking.

- To practice pressure free-throw shooting.

Description:

This game is a great exercise to teach aggressiveness with three players at a time. One offensive player is required to go against two defenders. The game begins with one player at the free-throw line shooting three shots. If the player makes all three shots, he keeps the ball and plays one-on-two from the top of the circle. If he misses any of the free throws, the ball is free to be rebounded by any of the three players who must take it back out to the top of the circle. Each player gets one point for a free throw, two points for a shot in the two-point area, and three points for a shot made behind the 3-point line. The winner is the first player to score exactly 31 points. If a player goes over 31, his score reverts back to 21.

If you are using the basketball boundaries as out of bounds, rotate possession in the same order as you did to begin the game. To make the game more aggressive, eliminate any boundaries and allow whoever gets the ball to keep it, regardless of where possession is obtained.

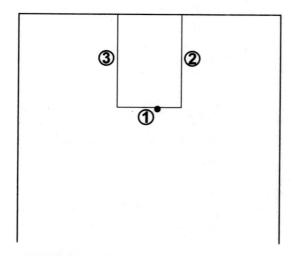

Diagram 87.

Drill 88 — First One to ...... for a Soft Drink

Objective:

- To provide players with an opportunity to engage in competitive games or simple contests for fun.

Description:

The coach can have a whole list of basketball-related challenges that he can use at the end of practice. Most of these ideas may not take any longer than ten seconds to a few of minutes. Once your players are used to hearing you say "First one to ......" , they will immediately come to attention for whatever challenge is coming next. The contest can be as simple as a single task or as complex as a series of skills or techniques.

It is nice to have some kind of reward for these types of challenges. For example, a single soft drink or a pack of gum, a popsicle, a pair of game socks, etc. will normally be all it takes to get your players excited and focused on the task at hand. Examples of fun challenges include:

First one to .....

- Name the emphasis of the day in practice.
- Name the terms we use to describe when defending a give-and-go.
- Name the words we use to communicate on defense when defending the post.
- Get a basketball and spin it on his finger for 10 seconds.
- Get a ball and make a basket at each hoop.
- Name all the starters on the local high school team.
- Make a three-pointer at both ends of the court.
- Bowl a basketball and hit a stationary ball at the far end of the court.
- Make a pass that hits a bulls eye.
- Correctly execute a screen and roll (partners).
- Correctly demonstrate a weak-handed lay-in.

You can use any physical skill or mental contest that you want, but it is a great time to reward listening, or to reinforce the value of a simple skill that was learned that day in practice. If you want players to carry over what they learned before, start your current practice with a question about something they learned during the previous practice.

Drill 89 — Domino Timed Passing Drill

Objective:

- To pass the ball and make lay-ins versus the clock.

Description:

Players line up in the posts as shown in Diagram 89. Using one basketball, they pass in sequence from O1 to O2 to O3 to O4 for a lay in. O5 rebounds and passes to O6, who then hits O7 for a lay-in. After they have passed, each player moves to the position they passed to, except O7, who moves to the end of the line, and O8, who rebounds and starts the next round. The players going for the lay-in cannot begin to move until the player passing to them has received the ball. As soon as your team has mastered the drill with one basketball, add a second ball, and then a third. Players will have to move very quickly after they have passed to be prepared for the next ball coming their way.

See how many lay-ins your team can make in one, two or three minutes. Keep an all-time best record. The more accurately and crisply they pass, the more shots they will make. Another way to test them is to see how long it takes to make a specified number of lay-ins (e.g., 30, 40 or 50), and then attempt to beat that time in the next practice. With younger players or the first few times you do this drill, it may be a good idea to place five marks on the floor where each player must begin in order to keep proper spacing.

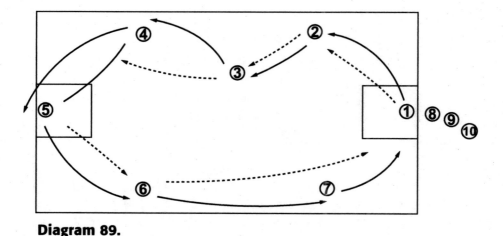

Diagram 89.

Drill 90 – Three Up

Objective:

- To practice pressure shooting.

Description:

Divide your team into two evenly matched groups and choose two equal-distance spots on the floor from where you want each team to shoot. Diagram 90 illustrates the teams shooting from the elbow. Each team has one basketball. The first player in line shoots the ball, and whether he makes or misses, he rebounds his shot and passes it back to the next person in his line. Players cannot intentionally interfere with either a shot or a pass from the other team. The goal is to get "three shots ahead" of the opposing team. If the blue team makes the first shot, and the red team misses, the coach calls "one up blue". If blue makes the next shot again before the reds, the call would be "two up blue". If the next shot that goes in is made by the red team, it goes back to "one up blue". The game continues until one of the teams gets "THREE UP". The winning team gets to choose the next shooting spot.

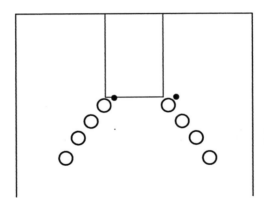

Diagram 90.

Possible variations to the drill include:

- Having two teams at each end play against each other, and then have winners vs. winners.

- Giving a reward to the player who hits the winning shot and to the player who made the assist to that shooter.

Drill 91 — Crazy Eights

Objectives:

- To practice pressure shooting and passing.

- To practice following your own shot.

Description:

Divide your team into three equal groups, each with their own basketball. Choose a shooting spot for each team approximately the same distance from the basket. This game is won by not getting points against your team. You get one point against your team every time the ball hits the floor after shooting a shot that misses. For example, if a player shoots a shot that misses, and before he can get to it, the ball bounces on the floor twice, that team has two points against them. If the shot goes in, no points are added if it hits the floor. As soon as a team gets eight points against it, they are eliminated, and the two remaining teams continue. The first person in each line shoots within three seconds of receiving the ball or it is point against them. Points can add up quickly if the ball is not rebounded in the air. After one team has won the game, rotate shooting spots.

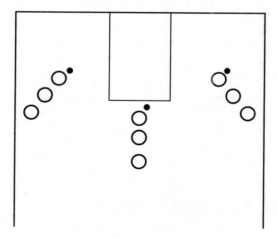

Diagram 91.

To add difficulty to this drill:

- Charge a point against a team if the ball is dropped on a pass back to the next shooter.

- Charge a point against a team if the ball hits the floor even on a made shot.

Drill 92 — 3-on-2 Continuous

Objectives:

- To practice fast-break reads, decision-making, and finishing.

- To improve fitness and stamina.

- To practice defending the fast break.

Description:

Divide your team in half and place one team on each sideline. Three offensive players attack two defenders until they score, or turn the ball over. When the ball is secured by the defense, those two players go on offense with the next player from the sideline joining them as the outlet. Diagram 92a shows O1, O2 and O3 coming down against X1 and X2. As soon as they score or turn it over, X1 and X2 go on offense and X3 becomes their third offensive player receiving the outlet pass (Diagram 92b).

The first team to reach a specified number of baskets wins the competition. The goal of the offensive team is to get a good first shot and then to get the offensive rebound, 3-against-2. Another objective of the offensive team should be to not ever turn the ball over, since they always have a man open. Furthermore, the offensive team should usually get second chances because they have a one-man rebounding advantage.

Defensively, the two players really have to scramble to cover the three offensive players. Their first responsibility is to stop the ball and then see how many passes they can make the offense throw before shooting. The defense has to realize that in actual game conditions, defensive help would be coming quickly as their teammates are retreating.

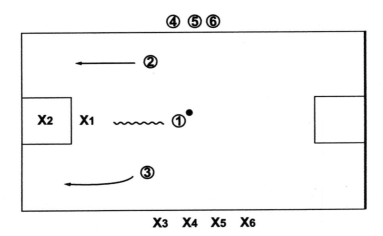

Diagram 92a.

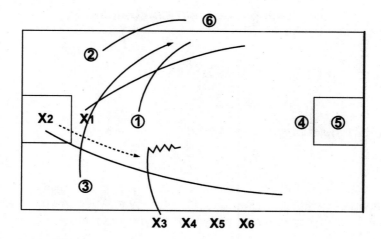

Diagram 92b.

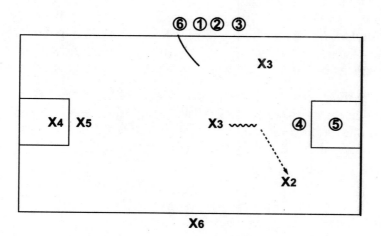

Diagram 92c.

Possible adjustments that can be made to this drill include:

- Placing only one defender back and bring in two defenders after the defender has gained possession to make it easier.

- Making the offense score on their first shot to make it more difficult.

- Allowing the third defender to come in as soon as the offense shoots (Diagram 92c). This could put the defender in a 3-on-3 situation if the offense gets a rebound.

- Allowing the third defender to enter the game on the first pass after the ball has passed half-court. This gives the offense less time to have an advantage and gives the defenders a goal of having to delay the offense only for a couple of passes so they can get to a 3-on-3 situation.

- Allowing the third defender to enter as the ball crosses the half-court line. This is the most game-like situation, and forces the offense to make quicker decisions.

Coaching Points:

- If the coach has the third defender enter before possession is gained by his teammates, it is a good idea to have him touch inside the center circle, so that he is entering the defensive end down the middle of the court, and also giving the offense a little more time.

- If the coach wants to speed up the tempo of the drill, he can require the offensive team to get their first shot up within a limited time after obtaining the ball (e.g., 5-to-10 seconds depending on their skill level).

- Teams can play to a specified number of baskets or for a specified amount of time (e.g., 3-to-10 minutes). Note: If players are moving quickly from end to end, as well as on and off the floor, this is a great conditioning drill.

Drill 93 – Sideline Basketball

Objectives:

- To provide players with the opportunity to participate in a controlled scrimmage.

- To enhance the conditioning level of the player.

Description:

Divide your team into two teams of six players each. Three players from each team are on the floor at a time. The other three players are located along their sideline, anywhere they choose. The sideline players can move up and down their sideline when they do not have the basketball. The players on the court are playing 3-on-3 full-court until one team scores. When either team scores, both teams exit the floor, and the next three from each team enter the court, with the team being scored upon bringing the ball inbounds. The players on the court can pass the ball to their sideline teammates at any time. The sideline players cannot shoot, but they can pass back to the players on the court or down their sideline.

The advantage for the offense is that they always have an unguarded pass to the sideline. The offensive team will learn to use the sideline when they have no other open passes, want to set a screen, or want to use a sideline pass as an outlet for a fast break. This game has a lot of end-to-end action. In order to keep the game moving, the coach can enforce a five-second time limit when the ball is on the sideline. The coach can balance the game by putting the strongest players from each team into the drill at the same time.

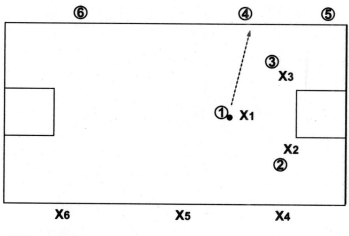

Diagram 93.

Drill 94 — 4-on-4 – No Excuses

Objectives:

- To practice playing pressure defense with no switching.

- To practice defending when mismatched.

Description:

This game can be played full-court or half-court. The goal is for each individual to stay on the floor and not be replaced. In order to stay on the court, a player cannot allow his assigned opponent to score. The eight players on the floor play a straight 4-on-4 basketball game, with all players matched up with the person defending them. Do not allow any switching, or excuses. If a player scores, the person guarding him exits the court to the end of the line, and the first person in line enters and guards the player who scored. For example in Diagram 94, if O2 scored, X2 would leave, and #9 would enter and guard O2.

The coach can use his discretion in "help situations" and fouling. This drill will often force players to defend a player who has a size or quickness advantage. The players are not allowed to make any excuses, thus teaching them to find a way to win their individual battle regardless of the conditions. If you are coaching offensive players who need to have a safety valve, you can be part of the offensive team as a passer only.

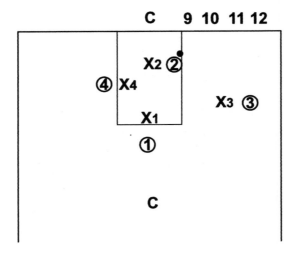

Diagram 94.

Drill 95 — Waves – 4-on-2, 4-on-3, 4-on-4

Objectives:

- To practice offensive decision-making.

- To practice offensive rebounding.

- To practice running the secondary break.

- To teach players how to scramble on defense when outnumbered.

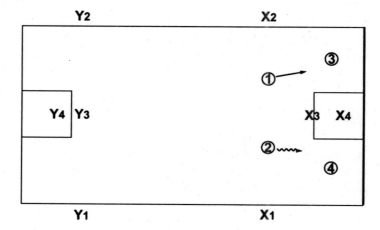

Diagram 95a.

Description:

Three teams of four players operate in "waves". For example in Diagram 95a, the X team begins on defense with X1 and X2 on the sidelines. As soon as X3 and X4 obtain possession of the ball, X1 and X2 come in to the outlet positions, and they go with the X team on offense against the Y team. After the Y team has gained possession, they go down against the O team, and the X team stays and waits on defense for the O's to come to them.

A coach can stay under each basket and inbound the ball, so that the defensive team can immediately convert to offense. The offensive teams are attempting to attack the basket with a two-person advantage. They can work on their secondary fast break pattern or simply attack when they have a numerical advantage. The offense should be able to score most of the time on either their first shot or by offensive rebounding 4-on-2 against the defense. The two defenders have to scramble to try to cover all four offensive players and protect the basket.

Diagram 95b illustrates the rotation after the X team has gained possession of the ball. The O team stays on that end of the floor, and O3 and O4 stay on defense, while O1 and O2 move to the sideline outlet positions. The X team breaks to the opposite end against Y3 and Y4. If the O team scored, the coach can inbound the ball to either X1 or X2.

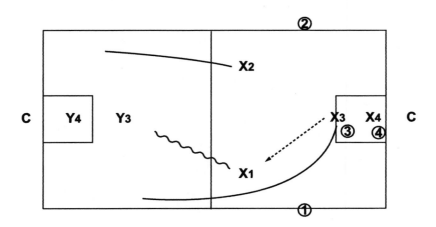

Diagram 95b.

Possible variations for this drill include:

- Giving the offense only a one-person advantage by going 4-on-3 with three defenders waiting for the offense.

- Bringing in all the defenders and go 4-on-4; this option is the best way to practice your secondary fast break pattern.

- Placing the four defenders in a diamond or a box formation to practice breaking against a zone.

- Going 4-on-2 and having the other two defenders come in on the first shot, passing over half-court first, or as the ball crosses half-court (similar to Drill 92) can make this drill more game-like.

Note: If you are carrying 15 players, this same drill can be run 5-on-3, 5-on-4 or 5-on-5.

Drill 96 – Defensive Game

Objective:

- To reinforce defensive principles by allowing the team to "score" by playing good defense.

- To force players to think and find ways they can score.

Description:

This game is played in the half court with either 4-on-4 or 5-on-5. The goal of the game is to score more points than the opponent. Points are awarded for the following factors:

The offensive team can score by:

- A basket = 1 point

- A shot in the key = 1 point

- An offensive rebound = 2 points

- A foul by the defense = 1 point

The defensive team can score by:

- A deflection = 1 point

- A steal = 1 point

- A defensive rebound = 1 point

- A charge = 4 points

- Good defense talk = 1 point

The game starts with a coin flip. The winning team can choose to play offense or defense first. The team that starts on defense stays on defense for three possessions and then switches to offense for three possessions. A team that is behind realizes that it can score regardless of whether they are on offense or defense and must find a way to get points. For example, an offensive team that is down by five, on the last possession, may try to get a shot in the key (1), intentionally miss to get an offensive rebound (2), miss again from inside the key (1) and go for a second offensive rebound (2) in order to win the game. A defensive team down by three can take a charge and win the game. Because scoring can become complex, it is a good idea to assign one coach to make judgements and another coach to keep score.

Drill 97 — Delay Game

Objectives:

- To practice an offensive delay game.

- To practice defending a delay game.

Description:

Similar to the defensive game, each team will get the same number of possessions on offense and on defense. In this game, a team can only score on offense. The goal of the defense is to prevent the offense from reaching any of their scoring methods. The methods the offense can use to score are as follows:

- Every ten passes without a turnover = 2 points.

- A made basket = 2 points and the same possession continues.

- If a foul is called, the offense gets to shoot an uncontested one-and-one and the same possession continues and the count of the number of passes begins where it left off.

- An offensive rebound = 2 points and the same possession continues.

For example, a team that makes 23 passes (4 points), then makes a basket (2 points), then makes ten more passes (2 points), gets an offensive rebound (2 points), and then turns the ball over after making 8 passes (zero points) will score 10 points on that one offensive possession.

The only way the defense can stop a possession is to get a defensive rebound, cause a turnover, or draw an offensive foul. If you want to practice "fouling the right player", you can adjust the rules to force the offensive player to make one or both free throws in order to maintain the same possession.

The coach may want to give teams a chance to huddle and plan their strategy between each possession. Coaches or captains can take responsibility for planning the strategy. The end of practice is the best time to schedule this drill. Just like in a game situation, the players have to make decisions and free throws while they are tired.

Drill 98 — 7-Second Shot Clock

Objectives:

- To practice full speed decision-making.

- To practice coming from behind when a team has to attack the basket and score quickly.

- To improve the players' level of physical conditioning.

Description:

Divide the squad in half and have the two teams play full-court. Everything is normal except that each time a team gains possession of the ball they have seven seconds to take a shot. Assign one coach the task of loudly counting down the shot clock every time the ball changes hands. The goal of each team is to score more points. The goal of each individual player is to stay in the drill for the whole time (three-to-five minutes). To prevent players from not sprinting from end to end, the coach can sub for any player who does not make it to the defensive end before a shot is taken. Being taken out of the game is usually a sign that the player is not in good running condition.

This drill will help identify the following factors:

- Players who can and will continue to get good "take-offs" for the fast break.

- Those players who are consistently able to get back on defense to make it difficult for the offense to get a good shot in a short period of time (i.e., seven seconds).

- Who has the stamina and determination to go to the boards.

- Who can make good judgements with the ball when they are tired.

Possible variations for this drill include:

- Requiring that at least one pass is made after the ball has crossed half court if you find that most shots are being taken off the dribble.

- Having the player run this drill with NO DRIBBLING. If you want to really challenge them — any time the ball is dribbled or there is no shot is taken within seven seconds, simply have the player place the ball on the ground so the defensive team can pick it up and convert to offense.

Drill 99 — Full-Court Scramble

Objective:

- To build endurance and stamina.

- To practice decision-making while tired.

- To work on making good offensive and defensive transitions.

- To practice dealing with unplanned play situation.

Description:

Divide the squad into two teams playing a full-court game. A coach stands at half-court on each sideline. Every time a team gains possession of the ball from the other team, they must pass the ball to one of the coaches. The coach with the ball can throw the ball back into the game to EITHER team and to ANY player. When that player catches the ball, they attempt to attack their offensive basket.

One of the purposes of this drill is to practice quick changes of direction and transitions to both offense and defense. If the players are playing hard during this drill, they will not be able to last very long (two-to-four minutes). On the other hand, they can strive to build up the length of time they can play without losing their mental focus and physical abilities.

The coach can throw the ball back in the game to the player out in front of the break, to a non-ball handler to make them give it up, or right back to the team that just lost it in order to force a second transition. The coach can also just throw the ball up for grabs and make both teams react aggressively to gain control of the ball.

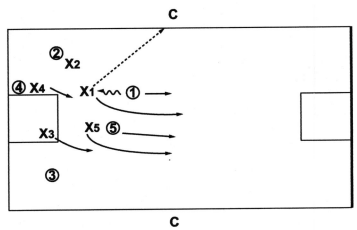

Diagram 99.

Drill 100 — The Shark Tank

Objective:

- To practice controlling and protecting the ball on the dribble.

Description:

This drill is an enjoyable exercise for players of all ages. Place half of the squad in *the shark tank,* (a confined area inside the key or inside the three-point line) at one end of the floor and half in the other end. Each player has a basketball. The six at each end are competing against each other. The goal of the game is continue dribbling while you knock the other players' basketball away from them and completely out of the shark tank. If a player recovers his ball and controls it before it goes out of the tank, he is still in the battle.

Players need to keep their heads up and protect the ball with their body to avoid losing their basketball. Once their ball is out of the tank, they are eliminated. The game continues until there is only one player remaining at each end. Then, the lone *sharks* left at each end come to the center circle and compete for the championship in a one-on-one battle to the end.

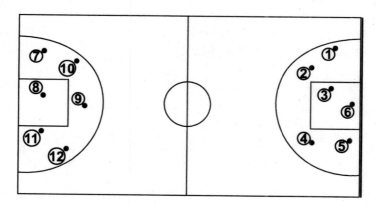

Diagram 100.

Drill 101 — End of Game Situations

Objective:

- To competitively practice offensive and defensive execution at the end of game situations.

Description:

Give your team a situation. Put one team on defense and one team on offense and allow them a one-minute "time out" to discuss what they are going to attempt to do. Depending on the age of your team and the leadership abilities of the players, this drill can be conducted with or without a coach. If you are going to allow the players to do the planning, it is interesting for the coach to silently listen in on the huddle to see who talks and what is said.

After the time-out, play the situation out to conclusion. Come together and discuss what was done correctly and what could have been done better or differently with both teams. Then, repeat the same situation with the same offensive and defensive teams. Again, meet and discuss the situation, and then *reverse roles* and play it out two more times. This drill will give your players and coaches confidence to have been through this situation before it happens in a game.

Things to include in a description of a situation are:

- The score.

- The amount of time remaining.

- Who has the ball.

- How many time outs each team has left.

- Where the ball is going to be inbounded.

- What the foul situation is.

Sample situations:

- Team A is ahead by four points with 30 seconds to go and the ball out of bounds at half court. Team B has only five team fouls against them and team A has committed 10 team fouls. Both teams have two timeouts remaining.

- Team A down by 10 points, three minutes to go, shooting a double bonus, three timeouts.

- Team B is up ten, in a one-and-one after two more fouls, no timeouts.

Bonus Drill – Down by a Hundred

If you have read this far you must really enjoy coaching, so here is a bonus drill for an enjoyable way to end practice. Have fun.

Objective:

- To practice shooting under pressure

Description:

Divide your team in half, with half shooting and half rebounding. Use the scoreboard and put the team score as Home – 0, Visitors – 100. Give your team a specified amount of time (three-to-five minutes), and tell them they get one point for every basket they can make in the time that is allotted. Have the manager on the scoreboard record every basket that is made as soon as time is started. When half the time has expired, the coach calls "switch" and the rebounders become shooters and vice versa. The goal is to make more than 100 shots and win the game. Coaches will have to make adjustments on the length of shots to give their players a legitimate chance to make more than a hundred. With high school and college players, we use the three-point line. You will find your players really pulling together to help the team reach this goal and come back from being down by a 100 points.